Praise for Who Cares What the Numbers Say

"Nonfiction writers face a sticky choice: to confide in the reader or confess to the reader? Julia Burns beautifully, artfully—often humorously—balances both. She confides and confesses, and the honesty of her words strikes at the heart of the nonfiction writer's goal to always to write the truth."

—Scott Mason,
WRAL-TV's *Tar Heel Traveler*
Author of *Faith and Air: The Miracle List,*
and *the Tar Heel Traveler* book series

"It was a privilege to walk alongside Julia in her journey, and I commend her for her bravery in writing *Who Cares What the Numbers Say?*"

—Sharon Guyer

"This is an inspiring account of going through hard times with a real faith that trusts, struggles, relies, leans in, questions but ultimately grows deeper. Julia truly builds her house upon the rock of God. We are inspired to walk through our own lives more intentionally learning the lessons God has for us."

— Helen Sawyer

"An honest look at one woman's life with cancer. Dr. Burns shares her fears, faith and pain as she seeks to live a purposeful life dispite the odds. I cried, I laughed and am asking myself some hard questions about my own life. Highly recommend!"

— Pat Horton

"Julia's lyrical style of writing catches one's breath with its crystalline precision. As an alongside witness to this season of Julia's life, I am struck at the raw-real so relatable in her writing which was so well-managed in her day-to-day interactions with us. Julia reveals the wrestling with the double-sided coin of suffering and hope and gifts the reader with the understanding required to find life-giving compassion."

—Kathy Parker

"A most moving reflection on human experience and Grace from a full grateful heart and the Holy Spirit, and the best preparation imaginable for our eternal journey together. Truly a wonderful piece of writing."

—Doug Monroe
Executive Director
Praxis Circle, Inc.

"A profound and honest account of Dr. Burns' experience with breast cancer. Her faith and belief in her own healing are deeply moving. Her perspective as a provider turned patient is full of wisdom and insight. An inspiring and unique read for anyone whose life has been touched by cancer."

—Jennie Petruney, MSN, ANP-BC, AOCNP
Duke Cancer Institute

Who Cares

what the

Numbers Say?

a journey in defying cancer

Who Cares

what the

Numbers Say?

a journey in defying cancer

JULIA W. BURNS, MD

Light Messages
Torchflame Books

Durham, NC

Published 2021, by Torchflame Books
an Imprint of Light Messages Publishing
www.torchflame.com
Durham, NC 27713 USA
SAN: 920-9298
Paperback ISBN: 978-1-61153-401-6
E-book ISBN: 978-1-61153-402-3
Library of Congress Control Number: 2021903900

For
Andy
&
Wilton Gray

I love God

I love God because he listened to me,
listened as I begged for mercy.
He listened so intently
as I laid out my case before him.
Death stared me in the face,
hell was hard on my heels.
Up against it, I didn't know which way to
turn; then I called out to God for help:
"Please, God!" I cried out. "Save my life!"
God is gracious—it is he who makes things
right, our most compassionate God.
God takes the side of the helpless;
when I was at the end of my rope, he saved me.
I said to myself, "Relax and rest.
God has showered you with blessings.
Soul, you've been rescued from death;
Eye, you've been rescued from tears;
And you, Foot, were kept from stumbling."
I'm striding in the presence of God,
alive in the land of the living!
I stayed faithful, though bedeviled,
and despite a ton of bad luck,
despite giving up on the human race, saying,
"They're all liars and cheats."

What can I give back to God
for the blessings he's poured out on me?
I'll lift high the cup of salvation—a toast to
God! I'll pray in the name of God.
I'll complete what I promised God I'd do,
and I'll do it together with his people.
When they arrive at the gates of death,
God welcomes those who love him.
Oh, God, here I am, your servant,
your faithful servant: set me free for your
service!
I'm ready to offer the thanksgiving sacrifice
and pray in the name of God.
I'll complete what I promised God I'd do,
and I'll do it in company with his people,
in the place of worship, in God's house,
in Jerusalem, God's city.
Hallelujah!

—Psalm 116

Foreword

"Fewer than one-quarter of survey respondents indicated they incorporate cancer prevention practices into their daily lives."

"THIS FINDING RAISES CONCERNS about the current state of cancer prevention in America, and strongly supports the need for more education on the topic, beginning at a young age." The survey—conducted online between July 9 and August 10, 2019—included 4,001 adults (53 percent women, 63 percent white) plus an oversample of 814 adults with cancer, for a total of 1,009 respondents (54 percent women, 83 percent white) who have, or previously had, cancer.

More than half (57 percent) of those surveyed expressed concern about developing cancer in their lifetime. However, only 24 percent indicated that they care deeply and incorporate cancer prevention practices into their daily lives. As a physician, the disparity in these statistics worries and astounds me. As a psychiatrist, I understand. No one works on preventing their death when they can pretend it will never happen.

Sixty four percent (64 percent) agreed that it is hard to know the most important things to do to prevent cancer. Although most of those surveyed agreed that smoking cigarettes (81 percent), family history (69 percent) and sun exposure (63 percent) increase risk for cancer, fewer knew about other lifestyle factors that increase risk, including obesity (36 percent) and alcohol (31 percent).1

Although it's never too late to make healthy choices, it's most critical for young people to take action to reduce their cancer risk because it can take decades for the disease to develop. I was fifty-seven when I received my diagnosis, and hoping I would live for decades, I combined traditional treatment with integrative practices and thrived.

Introduction

REMEMBER THE LAST TIME YOU HAD THE FLU and you were leaning over the toilet? That's perfect concentration, meditation on one specific point: *Please make it stop.* Nothing distracts you or diminishes the power behind the one obsession you hold sacred. *Let that be the last time. Make me well.*

When you're handed a death sentence by doctors who want to make you comfortable, that same attention comes into play. All you can think of is, *Noooo! This is not my life. This is not happening. I am not ready to die.* Or as a bright, young Christian speaker said, "Everybody wants to go to heaven, but nobody wants to go right now."

"Please, come pray for me. I'm dying." I grabbed my minister's hand between services two days after my biopsy, and we prayed for wisdom and faith, for the doctors to be wrong, for the cancer not to be so determined to live, snuffing out my life in the process. "Why God? Why me? Why now? Why aggressive, rare, and systemic?"

Living with the fear of dying mandates laser focus of both intention and attention. Loving and worshipping God and serving others requires that same focus, yet too often we drift toward chaos and distraction, away from peace and a simple life of obedience. God calls us back, faithfully.

Thankfully, a friend came over to pray and speak hope over me. "I don't think the way you think. The way you work isn't the way I work. God's Decree. For as the sky soars high above earth, so the way I work surpasses the way you work, and the way I think is beyond the way you think" (Isaiah 55:8-9, The Message). "Forget the question why, Julia. Focus on healing and wholeness. I declare the light of God falling over you and sustaining you with his Holy Spirit."

Ask others to pray also, but only if they can hold you healed and well. I did this and so much more, and was nurtured by the Holy Spirit. You can be, too. This book details some practices that facilitate returning attention to God, to the power, grace, and mercy of the Trinity. To the healing flow of His everlasting love.

I hope it helps you dance with the divine, and that light courses through you as you read these words, bringing you to completeness.

The Groan

"The mystery of creation is still groaning in one great act of giving birth...as we ourselves groan, waiting for our bodies to be set free."
—Romans 8:22-23

PAUL WROTE THESE WORDS IN A LETTER FROM PRISON to his friends in Rome. Unfortunately, it looked like my body was going to be set free sooner than I could have imagined.

The Internet Diagnosis

From: Julia Burns
Subject: Mastitis
Date: March 19, 2014
To: Lisa C, MD

Julia here with a medical problem. I have had mastitis since early February, which has not responded to two rounds of antibiotics. IT HURTS!! My doctor is trying to get me an appt. with the breast clinic, but I haven't heard anything since Monday.

It's started hurting more (sharp stabbing pain), and now I'm beginning to worry about Inflammatory Breast CA (bc I've been reading on the Internet). Who do you think I should see about this? I leave March 30, for two weeks to visit my son in Hong Kong and India, and would really like to have a specialist take a look before I go.

Thanks for the consult!!!

Julia W. Burns, MD

Prophecy

AND SO MY PROPHETIC POWERS LED ME ON A JOURNEY I had no intention of taking. I was expediting my trip to the cancer clinic, while at the same time I was sure I had a stubborn infection. Listening with both ears to different tunes, I believed in one, but also headed toward the other.

From: Julia Burns
Subject: Re: Mastitis
Date: March 21, 2014
To: Lisa C, MD

Good morning Lisa!

Thanks so much for checking in. I did get a call from Amy. I called her back this morning leaving my name & DOB.

I'm sure she will call back soon. I can come in any time.

Thanks,

Julia W. Burns, MD

From: Julia Burns
Subject: Re: Mastitis
Date: March 21, 2014
To: Susan

Yes, this time is good.

Any time is good.

I will prioritize this.

Thanks again,

Julia

From: Susan
Subject: Re: Mastitis
Date: Mar 21, 2014
To: Julia Burns

Susan wrote:

Thank you and I hope all turns out
well.

Susan

Message: If you feel there is something wrong with your body, keep searching. Do not listen to your doctor until you are satisfied with your diagnosis. Consult other doctors until you have a treatment plan that benefits you physically and emotionally.

The Biopsy

LOOK, I DON'T DRINK MUCH. I DON'T DRINK SODA. *I exercise an hour a day. I don't eat many carbs, sugar, or dairy, except when I'm cheating. My children have never seen me eat fast food. I keep my cell phone away from my body so the EMFs don't radiate me. Surely, you've got the wrong breast,* I pleaded silently, and unconvincingly.

The hard red knot that looks just like mastitis was looming between us.

"Check my husband's breast. Look, he's the one with his cell phone in his shirt pocket. Surely it isn't my breast you're looking for?"

But it was mine.

My provider, the one doing the biopsy, teared up, telling me that maybe I should have a drink or two tonight since I'm under "all this stress."

"Didn't you notice that huge lump under your arm?"

"Yes," I said, "but I thought it was a swollen lymph node since I had an infection." And I was still thinking, *What is she talking about? She's the one that looks stressed. I'm going to Hong Kong.*

And it's back down to the ultrasound suite for another

guided biopsy, and two oncology fellows that continue to tell me that if antibiotics worked some, then there is a chance it is infectious. But now I don't believe them. I'm thinking of the doctor upstairs that sent me downstairs with tears in her eyes. I'm holding back the tears in mine.

From: Julia Burns
Subject: Thank you
March 21, 2014
To: Lisa C, MD

Just finished in mammo, and waiting for surgeon to do skin biopsy. Can't thank you enough for expediting this.

My family practitioner ordered consult through another hospital, not UNC.

Julia

From: Lisa C, MD
Subject: Not mastitis after all
March 21, 2014
To: Julia Burns

Sure. Happy to help. Keeping my fingers crossed. Hopefully this will be resolved quickly.

L

Infection?

BUT QUICKLY WAS NOT IN THE CARDS. Prayers and crossed fingers weren't sufficient. The diagnosis came back inflammatory breast cancer, a rare and aggressive disease that spreads rapidly like an infection, but kills like cancer. Months of treatment was prescribed.

I waited a week before going to the doctor. My family physician treated an "infection" with two rounds of antibiotics. The six-week delay, and the breast clinic at another hospital that did not receive the urgent consult, allowed time for the tumor to grow. It was large and raging. The inflammation was deep, and stagnation in my lymph had created a six-by-nine-centimeter tumor with multiple painful nodes under my arm.

One minute you are riding to the hospital for a routine diagnostic mammogram to check out a pesky infection that has failed to clear with two rounds of antibiotics. And the next you are being poked and rolled and biopsied and stuck, and your skin punched until even with your meditation and breath skills you are saying, "Ouch. Yes, that hurts." And they say, "It's over."

But it's not. Not really.

It's just beginning.

"I'm leaving in a few days to see my son. After touring Hong Kong, we're going to that white love palace in India— the Taj Mahal," I tell everyone who touches me that day.

And without batting an eye, the surgeon says, "I'll write you a letter that will take care of your airline and hotel expenses."

Take care of what? You're not writing me any letters. I'm going to Hong Kong, I want to tell her, but now I'm more uncertain.

Message: Once you have a diagnosis, listen to your doctors. They will give you options for treatment, and you will have some decisions to make. Pay attention. Choose wisely the plan that works for you. Take your time.

Comfortable or Uncomfortable

AFTER FIRST CLEARING MY LIVER FOR CHEMOTHERAPY, my doctors reversed that opinion.

"There's something suspicious on your liver, and we have to re-image it to see if you're a candidate for treatment. If not, we'll keep you comfortable."

They got my attention when they talked about *metastatic cancer in the liver,* and *we can keep you comfortable.*

We waited seventy-two hours for the call that would determine the course of the year—comfortable or uncomfortable? We were counting on discomfort.

"I do love you, you know," said my stoic and extremely uncomfortable husband.

A pizza lay between us, uneaten.

"Ha," I replied. "I have to get cancer for you to say it."

New Englanders show love through actions not words. It was a point of dissension between us. One that seemed exceedingly trivial now.

Message: Waiting for clearance to receive treatment is torturous. Keep loved ones close by, and trust that treatment will be an option. Pray for God to continue to cover you with his grace. Believe in good news until bad news arrives. Don't make negative predictions unless you can predict the future—which, of course, no one can.

From: Julia Burns
Subject: Not mastitis after all
March 25, 2014

Hello, Julia here,

Hoping to hear today about the MRI and biopsy. Wondering about the chemo schedule. I have psychotherapy patients scheduled all day Wednesday and Thursday.

Julia

From: Lisa C, MD
Subject: Not mastitis after all
March 25, 2014
To: Julia Burns

I am so sorry about all this. Let
me introduce you to our wonderful
navigator. Once the details of the
timing and surgeon get worked out, she
will be your point person.

L

From: Julia Burns
Subject: Not mastitis after all
March 28, 2014
To:Lisa C, MD and Susan

Good afternoon,

I have not heard about the MRI. I tried
to call the breast clinic but could not
get through to a person.

Julia

Message: Be persistent. No one cares about your case
more than you.

The Results

CHEMOTHERAPY WAS DELAYED until the radiologist could clear my liver. They didn't want to put me through the suffering if it had already metastasized, and so we waited. It took three long days for the MRI results—the determiner between keeping me comfortable, and treatment.

Finally, we were given an appointment to come in, meet my team, and get the results of the MRI. That day held more waiting because they "lost" us in the waiting room. We were sitting right there by the oncology clinic sign, anticipating the announcement of my name. But they said they couldn't find us, that the receptionist—the one that was to ask my birthdate and if I have a port every week for the next seven months—told them we went to lunch. How they thought we could eat is beyond me. It took two hours before they found us, still sitting in front of the receptionist. Not eating.

They weren't looking forward to the meeting any more than we were.

We gathered in the smallest room—surgeons, residents, nurses, attendings, nurse practitioners, and a scheduler. It was crowded in there, filled with dire predictions and fear. Everyone's, not just mine.

The verdict came in. Whatever those spots were on my liver, they were deemed not cancerous, or no longer there.

"Tell me about your trip," my oncologist said, with all the compassion she could muster.

Shifting the conversation to Cytoxan and Taxol, she said, "We'll have to see how you tolerate it, if your feet and hands go numb."

After receiving a chemo schedule, I changed my work days to Monday and Tuesday. So for the next twenty-four Wednesdays, my husband and I drove across town and circled that huge parking lot, trying to find a space. Then we walked inside the cancer center, waiting until they hooked up the cocktail of the day.

But not before I prayed—over the chemo bag, the infusion nurse, other patients, myself, and my family. Nothing happened until after that.

"Lord, give me grace to accept this malady. Courage to believe in these doctors, nurse practitioners, and medications. May these chemicals attack the cancer cells and spare the healthy ones, minimizing negative side effects. May the light of your countenance shine down upon us, now and always. Protect my children from this tragedy. In the name of Jesus— the great Healer, the great Physician—we pray. Amen."

> **Message:** Nothing is too small for God. Ask Him to cover you with light so you don't fear. There is so much to worry about—try to stick to the facts. Don't project disasters, or you will paralyze yourself with all the difficult possibilities.

I Can't Come to Hong Kong

HOW DO YOU TELL YOUR SON YOU'RE NOT GOING to visit him in Hong Kong, when he is upside down and a day ahead? Carefully, we decided, not wanting to scare him, because we were scared to death.

Does that mean the diagnosis came on Saturday instead of Friday, the twenty-second and not the twenty-first, since Hong Kong is a day ahead? I hope so, because that gives me an extra day of health—an extra day of innocence.

When we called to tell Andrew I wasn't coming, he was watching seven-minute rugby matches, cheering for his team to win. It was a bright sunny day in Hong Kong, a big party coming at the end of this athletic competition.

I want to do that, too—cheer for a victory, celebrate with a party.

> **Message:** Celebrate as much as you can. Look for good, and hold your loved ones close as you wait for your treatment to start. Be truthful with your trusted family and friends so they can support you.

Travel Plans

It's been ten days since I found out. Strange how fast your world contracts when a diagnosis takes you into weeks of chemo, followed by surgery and radiation.

I feel so far away. So much further than if I had actually gone to Hong Kong and then India. Before the diagnosis, I was researching our trip to the Taj Mahal, determining transportation, emailing Sachi, our Rotary Exchange daughter, to see if she wanted to go with us. Sachi lives in Gujarat, and we were planning a reunion. Her family wanted to thank us for watching out for her during her year in America.

While planning our itinerary, I noticed the Taj Mahal was closed on Friday.

"We can't go to the Taj Mahal on Friday. It's closed, and we wouldn't want to cross the country to find ourselves locked out of that beautiful palace."

That building embodies such an amazing love story about a king so enamored with his wife that he built the white palace in her honor. Then he was imprisoned by his son because he wanted to build another white palace to honor her once more. His adoration almost bankrupted the country.

Now I wonder about another love story. One where a husband sits for eight hours in the waiting room of an oncology hospital, wondering, *What could be taking so long?*, and *When will they be finished draining his wife's abscess?* His cell phone was not working, and his tablet was out of juice, so he couldn't even distract himself with business calls and money matters.

Message: Remember to appreciate all the kindnesses you experience from your family, providers, and friends. Thank them. I remember reminding myself, *If I'm dying, I might as well have fun. If I'm not dying, I might as well have fun.* I stuck to that over the two-year course of treatment. Gratitude was an important tool in my repertoire.

Touch My Titties

MOMMA WAS SUPERSTITIOUS, and some of that rubbed off on me. I rarely told anyone about the diagnosis while inside my house. I didn't want those words sticking to the walls and being held captive there after I was healed. So I told folks on my deck, in cars, in restaurants, but rarely in my house. Most of my friends knew about the mastitis because sometimes the pain was so sharp I would catch my breath and gasp. When they asked what was wrong, I told them I had an infection.

Sally was the first friend I made when I moved to Chapel Hill seven years ago, and I told her from my car. We met through her daughter Cathy. She came to our house after meeting Wilton the first week of high school.

They hit it off, and Cathy went home and said, "Hey, you've got to meet the new girl's mom. She's nice. I think you'd like her."

That started a long friendship, and years later she helped me renovate and decorate a 1965 modernist home. It was a true and abiding friendship, the kind that allowed you to talk about paint colors, and *Should we really tear up all the old carpet?*

She also knew about my painful, pesky infection that didn't clear after weeks of antibiotics.

I told her because she kept saying, "How's your breast infection? Feeling better?"

She was a nurse, after all.

Instead of saying, *No, I feel much worse.* Finally, I called her from my car and said, "I have inflammatory breast cancer. I start chemo next week."

After much silence, she said, "Who's your surgeon?"

When I told her, she replied, "Ahhh. That man can touch my titties any day. Julia, he's the best surgeon, and so good-looking."

At first I was stunned, but then I laughed out loud. Bottom-of-the-stomach laughter filled my car. How good to have a friend that can joke about mastectomies and good-looking surgeons. And she also organized volunteers who provided meals for my family for the next six months.

> **Message:** I found it was best to be honest with friends. When they asked questions, I answered to the best of my ability. If I couldn't answer, I told them so. Without confiding in Sally, I would not have had weekly meals, or the support my family deeply needed. And I would have missed the best laugh ever.

Telling Patients

WHILE PRACTICING PSYCHIATRY in my home office, I had many patients who were receiving grief counseling and trauma healing. Each patient had a unique need to know the how, why, and when of this illness—an illness that could eventually separate us, even if I lived.

My plan was to discharge my grief patients and pediatric patients, and continue with my other adult patients. As an adult, child, and adolescent psychiatrist, my practice was wide-ranging. I enjoyed the diversity.

I wrote in my journal, "This cancer's my secret because I would never have one of my patients find out from the Internet."

The blog I started in 2012—when my daughter went to Thailand, and my mother died—was halted until I was able to tell each patient in person.

While I was waiting to begin the telling, one patient called to say that her father had passed away. She was still reeling from her husband's recent death from cancer. How do I speak this news into the phone? Or heaven forbid, sit close to her in my office and say that word *malignancy?*

"With God by your side," I heard the echo surrounding me. "With God, all things are possible."

This seems so unfair, though. I knew I couldn't continue to see her as my hair fell out and I became gaunt—watch her watching me, wondering how long before I left her, too. I want to hold her close and beg forgiveness for being yet another person to give way to the cells—undifferentiated growth thirsting for someplace to reside. Another body destroyed. It seems unkind to rob her once again of someone on whom she has grown to depend and love.

I won't do this to you, I long to say. *I won't ever get cancer. Or God forbid, ask you to watch while I wither away during chemotherapy, as you look for signs, fearfully remembering the countdown with others while you measure it out with me.*

And so this secret stayed a little while longer. The fewer patients I told, the less it intruded into my life. If I remained silent, could I halt this dark dance?

"Doctor Burns, how was Hong Kong?" my patients said. "I want to hear about your trip."

Since they would never believe that I took weekly trips to the hospital instead of a journey to Asia with my son, I remained voiceless.

Message: Telling co-workers or clients created another puzzle. I decided to wait until I had caught my breath and started treatment before telling all my patients. I discharged some because they had lost family members to cancer, but I continued to work throughout the two years of treatment. Each patient had a need to know, and to be taken care of individually.

Walking

I SIGNED UP FOR A FITBIT STUDY and walked six thousand steps, even on Wednesdays, my chemotherapy day—determined to be healthy and strong, despite the diagnosis and treatment. The hypothesis being tested was whether or not movement decreased nausea and other side effects of chemo. I was eager to participate, to help them prove that exercise improved outcome.

The research coordinator who registered me for the study had lots of questions. Most of them were easy. "How tall are you? How much do you weigh? Date of birth? How much do you exercise? How much pain are you in?"

Then she asked me how many weeks I'd be in treatment. But I didn't have an answer. Six months, one year, or until my hands and feet go numb? Whatever the correct answer, it seemed impossibly long and impossible.

Message: Here, I show despair about my future. Often, it is hard not to feel sorry for yourself, especially if your situation is uncertain.

Looking forward, I turned to optimism and shunned negative predictions. They only confused and hurt me.

Work

As I proceed through Cytoxan and Taxol infusions, I wondered if I should continue working. What did God want? What did I want? Was it time, after so many years of patient care, so many stories, to separate myself from others' pain and seek my own more clearly?

Without my patients, without my healing work, my wisdom and discernment, I was as lost as a paper boat bobbing down a creek, rudderless. My every breath was to heal and edify. This work defined me, and I was not ready to give it up, not yet hearing God say it was finished.

A brown rocking chair in my basement office held me as I listened. Each story spoken by a patient created sharing, a sacredness continuing in our give and take. This communion, this healing was comprehensive. I continued working as long as I could.

He holds in His hand
our own our life.
He holds in His hand
our breath.
Breathing being difficult sometimes,
remember this,
that when you inhale, you taste Him,
and when you exhale, He tastes you.

He holds in His hand
our all our life.
He holds in His hand
each of you.

When I breathed in, I tasted Him. When I breathed out, He tasted me. And so, breathing being difficult sometimes, we faltered. And after a particularly difficult session with a patient, I believed little had been accomplished, until I stopped and remembered, "Whenever two or three are gathered..."

After humbling myself and my expectations, I had faith that restoration was taking place in spite of my ingratitude and ignorance.

> **Message:** Continuing to work is a personal decision. Working allows you to be something other than a sick person with cancer. It creates a distraction and provides a purpose for living. However, if you are too sick to work, then a sabbatical or leave of absence might be best. Also, some jobs won't allow sick time, and you will be forced to quit.

Subdue the Grieving

WAKING AND WALKING IN THE WORLD with the constant pain of this rare, aggressive monster growing inside, changed my perception. The world appeared in technicolor. The birds were brighter, as were their songs. The sweet rounding of the creek slipped by with a shushing, shurring rhythm that caught my imagination. Hawks were gliding over and under, over and under once more, in a surreal dance. Even the rain was louder and unrelenting, loosening the roots of a large oak tree, and slamming the trunk to the banks of the creek behind my house. It rested there beside a hollow birch.

I painted this birch many times after Momma died, singing this song as I created.

When a soul flies out of its temple,
it seeks the solace of the water's curling.
Repetitive rhythms ring the shore,
calling a spirit closer
to subdue the grieving
the left behind loved ones
must endure.

Written for my godfather on the occasion of his death, I sang this song and painted the birch on the occasion of Momma's. Now it seemed someone might be singing and painting for me.

Message: The world lights up on the occasion of a terminal diagnosis. It is God's way of assuring you that you have lived an existence of beauty and privilege, and that He will never forsake you. He knows the number of hairs on your head, and He sends the sights and sounds to reassure you.

My Secret

> *"All that I have seen teaches me to trust the*
> *Creator for all that I have not seen."*
> —Ralph Waldo Emerson

LIVING AND BREATHING IN THE ASSURANCE of the Creator's wisdom while planning, I sang, *"Thy will be done on earth as it is in heaven."* It was my thanks to God, remembering that I was not in charge as I once wanted.

Not liking the abuse stories I was hearing when I was medical director of a three-hundred-child welfare agency, I thought I could do better than God. As I demanded safety for my pediatric patients, even as they sang their abuse stories, it seemed He wasn't listening. After years of pleading with God to change humanity and create safety for children, I despaired in a loving God.

Now I was pleading for my own safety. As the cashier bagged my groceries, I marveled at each healthy person, watching folks closely. They looked, but didn't see. And I was glad for the extra week where their glances did not reveal my disease—my hair, still full and brown, with little gray.

I pondered the young mother that raced past with her toddler, on the way to the bathroom, knocking into my port in her haste. She'll never know the hurt she gave. Neighbors walked down our road, beside their dogs, as I walked with mine. We bantered back and forth, to and fro. Cherishing these last freedoms, I knew that soon the chemo would take its toxic turn and announce my disease. With my balding head, these private chats—these precious, simple conversations—would cease.

Discerning everything and everyone as miraculous, the world vibrated in a radiance so pure and lovely it was easy to feel God's love and support. If I covered my port and venous access line, no one knew. Not yet.

Message: Let the world vibrate for you in its radiance, and dance with the Holy Spirit. Remember, no matter how much advice people give you, this is your journey, your story. You decide who gets to know about your treatment, and when. And although it is important not to isolate yourself, it is also important to be the director of your story. Of course, if your hair falls out, people will know. But you get to choose whom you allow to accompany you to treatment.

Dire Predictions

THE INTERNET DID NOT HELP.

"Don't google this illness unless you want the pants scared off you," I told my friends and family.

Looking at the grim data, I saw that it was collected in 2008. That meant the study began around 2004, a decade ago. Hoping I would live that long—a decade—I wanted to be the statistic that fell to the longer side of the graph.

As I stared at my computer, I did not want to believe the graph that showed less than a 25 percent chance of living two years. I wanted to survive. I wanted to go to Hong Kong.

Message: Take care not to search the Internet for information about your prognosis and disease. Let your doctors lead you toward the knowledge you need. Be optimistic, no matter what the projected outcome. You can be the master of your journey, asking God to protect you and heal you from all unhealthy cancer cells. Protect your friends and family, too. They need to be positive about you when they pray.

I'm Tired

AND SO THIS NEW DAWN, THIS DIFFERENT WAY OF LIVING, was upon us, thrust down, calling my name, Dr. Julia W. Burns, and altering my life entirely.

One day, I got a diagnosis and googled it and started praying that I wouldn't die. The next week, I started chemotherapy and did well.

"Wow, you are doing fantastic, walking six thousand steps and no nausea."

Still I wondered how I was going to survive with a rapidly advancing cancer that must die if I am to live. If it's inside of me, weren't they killing the good and the bad, the healthy and the diseased? Imagine the awfulness of those chemotherapy toxins as they crawled around, attacking.

A war raged inside my armpit, where a lymph node the size of a kidney bean throbbed. Deep stabbing pain penetrated as I tried to kill it, instead of it killing me. Each week, my white blood cell count lowered, so I had to take a shot that made my mouth taste like metal, curling my tongue and my right hand. The hand that painted and wrote now shook constantly. I rolled into a ball on the sofa and held very still, because moving triggered a bone-deep aching, and I wondered if I had the flu. But it turned out that this miracle injection that costs thousands of dollars caused flu-like pain, even as it increased my white blood cell count.

Counting the number of shots and treatments I had left, I wondered how I'd survive. And I was tired. Tired of everyone telling me how great I look, how amazing I am, and how it's all going to be fine in a year.

A year is a very long time.

> **Message:** Remember that when you feel tired and sick, it's easy to be negative. When you don't feel well, it is hard to dispel thoughts of death and the months left for treatment. Try to put things into perspective. This time will pass. Let others pray for you. Believe what they tell you—that you look good, strong, and that you are going to feel better soon. You will come out of this dark hole.

Losing Hope

PART OF ME WANTED TO GIVE UP so that folks would never know the disconnect I felt from my own healing. My body was messaging me daily about death. Moment by moment, this strange stabbing ached on the right where they said the cancer was shrinking, but it felt like it was growing.

It hurts so much. I don't want to die. I don't want to live like this. I don't want my children or patients to know this pain. I don't want anyone to have to read this, but I must write or I'll wither away. And I don't want to do that either.

> **Message:** Journaling can be a key component to your health journey as a place where you can safely talk about your fears and voice your concerns. Since it is hard to discuss some things with your family and friends, your journal can be a safe haven. You can choose whether or not to read the entries, or tear them out and burn them. They belong to you.

Don't Tell Me

YEARS BEFORE BEING DIAGNOSED with breast cancer, I read a book about women of the Bible which placed depression in an unfavorable, but predictably old and untenable, position.

The author stated, "It is true that depression is related to the way we think—or fail to think—about God. Once we bind ourselves to a God-sized God, we have a resource for dealing with depression. We can focus on God—His holiness, His knowledge, His power. We can face our fears and anxieties in the light of His character and His commitment to us. If depression results from the way we think about ourselves, then it can be lifted by the way we think about ourselves in relation to a holy, knowledgeable, and powerful God who is committed to us. The downward look is what leads to depression. The upward look takes away our fear. Look to God."

Here was my response: I am going to rewrite that paragraph and change just one word. I am going to substitute *breast cancer* for *depression*. See how it reads now: "It is true that breast cancer is related to the way we think—or fail to think—about God. Once we bind ourselves to a God-sized God, we have a resource for dealing with breast cancer. We can focus on God—His holiness, His knowledge, His power. We can face our breast cancer in the light of His character and His commitment to us. If breast cancer results from the way we think about ourselves, then it can be lifted by the way we think about ourselves in relation to a holy, knowledgeable, and powerful God who is committed to us. The downward look is what leads to breast cancer. The upward look takes away our breast cancer. Look to God."

This wide-sweeping proclamation restricts our treatment options, making it unholy to accept a biological basis for depression. The writer asserted that depression was not only caused by how we think, it was caused by our relationship to God. She was prescribing a change in our attitude to God, not a trip to the psychiatrist for therapy or medication. Rewriting the paragraph to change the word depression to breast cancer makes it seem ludicrous. I could have used other biological illnesses, substituting ulcers, headaches, GI, thyroid, or brain cancer.

Clearly, we understand that biological illnesses have a spiritual and emotional component. If this is so, why can't we make the leap that mental and emotional illnesses have not only a spiritual and psychological component, but a biological one as well?

"We live in a country that reimburses for gastric bypass,

but not for psychotherapy," I say, frequently. Western thinking causes great harm as we cut the head from the shoulders and continue to wonder at the rising rates of cancer, mental illness, drug and alcohol addiction, STDs, shooting sprees, and suicide.

A recent study reports that ER visits for suicidal ideation have doubled for middle schoolers, from 2009 to 2015 (five hundred thousand to 1.12 million).2 And yet we continue to fund studies that measure the causal relationship between violent video games and aggression, suicide, and homicide3. And we wonder how digital access to pornography is changing the way our teenagers relate to each other. We are desperate to find meaningful connections to each other and God, and social media is failing us.

I have a grievance with this Christian writer, who attempts to convince us that mental illness, psychological pain, and suffering is somehow related to our relationship with God. I wish one sexually abused, anxious, depressed woman or man would come to my office not feeling like they caused their abuse. That one patient would come in depressed and angry about being abandoned by God instead of feeling guilty that they in their sinfulness had abandoned God first.

When I retired as medical director of a three-hundred-child welfare agency, feeling numb, confused, sad and frustrated, I was also angry—really angry that I had believed in a God who allowed such destructive human relationships. It wasn't 1–2 percent of people who suffered from sexual abuse in childhood, as I had been taught. It was 25 percent of children, and a significant number of young children required psychiatric treatment or institutionalization. I was furious and blamed God.

Anger nearly destroyed me, until finally, after reconciling with God, I realized that it was humans who created sin and suffering, while God witnessed the carnage, weeping with each wounded individual.

When this popular, female Christian writer describes depression as a wrong relationship with God, she is sanctimonious and destructive. When will we accept that depression is genetic, biological, and treatable. That a trip to the psychiatrist is a sign of good mental health, not a reason to get turned down for health insurance?

Being in relationship with God makes every journey lighter and brighter, whatever illness or challenges may come. The hope and healing inherent in belief in a Higher Power is demonstrated by the millions who have been healed in Alcoholics Anonymous and healing prayer. Every day, miracles occur for the believer and the non-believer. But don't tell my patients who come for treatment of anxiety, stress, depression, trauma, and drug addiction that they are suffering because they aren't right with God. Those are words that judge and accuse, and the great Creator would never condone this view, because he loves us too much.

Message: Turn from people who give messages that you caused your cancer and can stop it if you change your thinking. They are wrong. You don't deserve lectures and opinions that create pessimism and pain. Think for yourself. Find books that uplift and elevate your mood and thoughts. Be independent. Love yourself enough to eschew theories of condemnation and fear.

Pray for Me

CHEMOTHERAPY WAS EXCITING AT FIRST, as I prayed for God to guide the medicine, target the cancer and not healthy cells, believing in the reversal of this growth. But now I am scared and worried about what more Adriamycin and Cytoxan treatments will do besides take my hair. And then sixteen weeks of Taxol, followed by radical surgery and radiation. How could I possibly be on the first weeks of a thirty-six-week journey?

Help me, pray for me, lift me up when I am too discouraged or weak to pray and meditate. Strength will be the answer. I will borrow yours when I am unable to find my own.

Message: I borrowed God's strength when mine was insufficient. I dove deep into the vigor and solitude of the Lord, and lifted up a feeble cry for help. "I've abandoned my hope, Lord. Save me," was all I could muster somedays, and yet it felt full and complete. I trusted Him to rescue me. And He did.

Injustice

SHORTLY AFTER THE DIAGNOSIS, I was at my little cousin's soccer game when a family practitioner asked me what kind of doctor I was. When I told him, "child psychiatrist," he replied, "Can I have a prescription for Adderall? My eight-year old won't practice his cello. Isn't that what these parents say to you?"

Wow! was all I could think, with this bitter response about medicating attention deficit disorder. He must have had a terrible experience. I didn't tell him about the fourteen-year old girl, Cassie, I saw last week. She came with suicidal ideation and depression, legal charges for shoplifting, and an incident in the emergency room with alcohol poisoning.

Lots of my patients have attention deficit hyperactivity disorder. Boys typically get treatment after hitting, biting, or kicking—misbehaving in a manner that gets them the response they desperately need. Well-behaved girls get left behind, spending years working and learning, studying and knowing lessons the night before the test. But not the next day during the test, because anxiety, combined with short-term memory and working memory deficits, cause them to forget. Labeled lazy and unmotivated, girls get diagnosed and treated less frequently than boys. So by junior year in high school, the work load is so unbearable that they give up, often refusing school and becoming depressed and suicidal.

The correct diagnosis and treatment ended Cassie's substance abuse and acting out, but imagine how much suffering could have been saved if she had come in earlier—perhaps in first grade, when she struggled with reading, and her comprehension was so poor she needed tutoring. Too bad she didn't play the cello.

> **Message:** Sometimes the diagnosis of attention deficit disorder is controversial. I am proud that I organized many young girls' lives and taught the patients and their families about the impulsivity, hyperactivity, and inattention that created chaos

for everyone. Often, psychoeducation and low-dose medication created a transformation that allowed the patient to flourish. I celebrated this and believed in my patients' ability to heal.

Thomas

I AM DISCHARGING MY PEDIATRIC PATIENTS. One of my favorites, Thomas, is a wondrous formation of God's incredible creative power.

"Doctor Burns, I'm so glad to see that you are supporting cancer." He looks at my balding head with confidence, intelligence shining.

His cleverness was clear from the first day we met, when he was two years old and he ran around the office, jumping on tables and furniture, singing as he knocked into others in his rush to get where he was going.

"Let's build another Lego tower after we finish Uno!"

He wanted more. Always more. His mind racing so far ahead of his ability to enunciate that he stuttered. So many thoughts and ideas rushing over themselves that they fell together and tripped his tongue.

"Uno! I win again," I said.

It was love at first sight for me, if not for him. And it wasn't for him. When the technician came into the room to get his blood pressure, he would have nothing to do with her or that. He was a moving target, and if you wanted to stay with him, you had to move, too. His parents were symbols of grace and patience as we started our path together, unfolding the secrets of his mind, maximizing his many strengths. But that ended yesterday.

"Doctor Burns, I'm so glad you are supporting cancer. I learned about it in school, that when you supporate others, you cut your hair. Good for you. I'm glad I'm here. I told Mom I want to see Doctor Burns because I need to de-stress. My stress and worry is worse on Wednesdays because I have to go to school and then baseball, and then I have church choir, and when I get home, I only have time to eat and go to bed. There is no time for homework on Wednesdays. And that is my stress. If I don't do my homework, then I worry and stress more, and I act out and cry and misbehave and don't do what I'm told, and then I am really worried and stressed. I need to de-stress badly."

Just like we have done since he was two, we talked about de-stressing. You have to listen hard to help him slow down and stop interrupting. It's a lot of work, but eventually he can do it.

He'd been going to aftercare and playing with his best friend instead of doing homework because it made his heart happy when he was playing, but not later when he was behind—tired and worried about not completing his work. He said he doesn't mind working in school, but that working after school was just too much, especially with other activities that he liked and didn't want to give up. He admitted that if he finished his work in aftercare, things went smoother. But the temptation to play was often overpowering. And on and on he talked, until he came up with his own de-stress plan while I sat there, listening. He's only nine, but he's so remarkable.

As the session came to an end, we were finishing our last game of UNO, which I won.

"But can't we play one more. You always win, and I want to."

I told him I had cancer and I wasn't just supporting it.

"Oh, that's too bad. I was hoping, really sure that you only liked to supportate it."

"I am going to receive many treatments. They will make me well, eventually. But in the meantime, my hair will fall out and I might be too sick to see you, Thomas. Your pediatrician can write your prescriptions."

He said, "I don't know what a pediatrician is, and I don't want to see them. I want to see you."

"Who do you see when you have a sore throat or stomachache?"

"My doctor."

"How about you see her in August, right before school starts, and then come see me in December, before or after Christmas, depending on how I'm doing?"

"No, I want to see you next week. I still need de-stressing."

I wrote his teacher a note: *Please grade Thomas's homework leniently on Thursdays.*

That made him happy, but he immediately started negotiating.

"How about I get to choose between Tuesday and Thursday, because sometimes Tuesdays are worse, too."

Knowing how quickly we get stuck in the quagmire of his bargaining, I replied, "We're going to let your mother and teacher, the adults, decide the details because they know more than I do."

Then it was time for him to leave.

"Know what, Doctor Burns?"

"No, what?"

"You know the saying, *slower than Christmas*?"

"Yes, I do."

"Well, this year, Christmas is going to be extra slow because I'm going to be waiting to see you. It's going to take a really long time this year, isn't it?"

What could I say but, "Yes, Thomas. A very long time indeed."

I cried when we hugged goodbye.

He said, "I'll miss you."

"We can speak on the phone," I whispered. "And your mother will call to see how I am."

I told my husband there are some things I would cry about, even if I didn't have cancer. Saying goodbye to Thomas is one of them.

Chemo Works Wonders

From: Julia W. Burns, MD
Subject: Headache
Date: April 3, 2014
To: Amy

Wow!

Big changes on tumor. Dense area
more compact and smaller. Thick gel
extension shrank also.

Boob much less tender and more jiggly.
Yeah!! Thanks.

Really happy! Joined Fit Bit and walked
6K steps after chemo.

What to I take for HA. Confused.
Tylenol or Advil?

Julia

From: Amy
Subject: Headache
Date: April 3, 2014
To: Julia W. Burns, MD

Good morning.

You may take either Tylenol or Advil
for the headache. Make sure you stay
hydrated and keep moving.

Glad to hear about the changes. Chemo
does work wonders.

Amy

From: Julia W. Burns, MD
Subject: Gene
Date: April 16, 2014
To: Amy

Forgot to ask about genetic link BRCA?
Wilton wants to know if she should get
tested.

Julia

From: Lisa C, MD
Subject: Gene
Date: April 16, 2014
To: Julia W. Burns, MD

Hi. You have a family history, although not a terribly strong one, so it would be reasonable to ask Genetics to evaluate. No emergency but since you're asking we can move that up.

Amy can you facilitate a referral?

Lisa

Message: There will be many tasks required of you during your cancer treatment that are difficult and sad. Face them head-on. If you have prayer support, make sure you let your prayer partners know ahead of time about these tasks, and have them cover you with prayer. Saying goodbye to Thomas was one of the most challenging tasks I tackled, as we had been together for years. Educating his parents and supporting them to help Thomas, who was brilliant but had many difficult behaviors, was one of the highlights of my career.

Name, Date of Birth

"NAME, DATE OF BIRTH," is the constant refrain, to which I reply, "Julia Burns, one, twenty-eight, 1957." This repetitive and impersonal ID check, the question never asked with eye contact, will hopefully keep me from receiving someone else's medication. And them, mine.

I wanted only my cocktail du jour. But by the time a saline hydration bag was hung, I was sobbing. A four-hour delay caused my breakdown. The new computer program failed, and if you can't enter drugs and bill, you can't proceed with treatment. Those hours in the waiting room, waiting for the computer program to reboot, depleted us.

Once we were in the infusion room, a baby hovered on the television screen, advertising diapers as my tears overflowed.

"Don't have a baby without me," I said to my daughter.

She had not missed a single infusion session.

"Please let me hold your babies."

Tears fell from both our eyes then. We were unsure of our future together, and so scared.

When the gauntlet fell, and the verdict came in guilty, the first thing I thought was, *I don't think I'll be able to take the waiting. The waiting rooms with all the people.* That was after praising God that Momma was dead, *because this would surely kill her.* Then I thanked Him for my black convertible, which I hadn't waited to have fun driving to the beach with the top down.

I am a solitary creature. I like to garden alone, read and write alone, walk through the forest alone. Sitting for hours with cancer patients in the waiting room surely seemed like purgatory. A different kind of death, but a funeral all the same.

But when it happened—the endless wait while the new computer system stalled—I stood up to it. Turns out, I can tolerate cancer, chemotherapy, sharp pains in my breast, and waiting rooms with hundreds of people. Noise-canceling headphones helped. And I made it.

Message: There will be times when challenges come unexpectedly. As always, I contacted my prayer partners for assistance. "Help. Pray for me. I'm stuck." And they always came through. Try to accept these trials, because they will certainly present themselves. Lean hard on the Lord, and your noise-cancelling headphones!

Hallelujah

From: Julia Burns
Subject: Shrinking!
Date: May 15, 2014
To: KP, HS, JW, SG PH

Dear prayer warriors,

My tumor shrank four centimeters. Finished the most toxic treatments and continuing on with the Taxol. See you tomorrow at 11 a.m. Thank you, thank you, thank you.

Julia

From: Kathy
Subject: Shrinking!
Date: May 15, 2014
To: Julia Burns

Praising God and thanking Him with you.

KP

From: Robert
Subject: Re: Shrinking!
Date: May 15, 2014
To: Julia Burns
Cc: Sharon, Kathy

For this reason, I bow my knees to the Father of our Lord Jesus Christ

to Him who is able to do exceedingly, abundantly above all that we can ask or imagine, according to the power (Holy Spirit) that works in us. To Him be the glory! Eph. 3:20.

Thank you, Jesus for this wonderful hope!"

PAXPLH

From: Sharon
Subject: Re: Shrinking!
Date: May 15, 2014
To: Julia Burns

PRAISE God. We rejoice with you.

SG

Prayer Chain

From: Julia Burns
Subject: Pray
Date: July 31, 2014
To: KP, HS, JW, SG PH

Two-hour wait for the doctor. Now, four-hour wait for infusion.

Please pray.

Haven't even started. Yuck.

Julia

My prayer team's responses:

From: From: Kathy
Subject: Pray
Date: July 31, 2014
To: Julia Burns

Lord, redeem the time.

You got this.

KP

From: Sharon
Subject: Pray
Date: July 31, 2014
To: Julia Burns

Dear Julia,

I hope the process got done and that you are OK.

Let us know.

Bless you!

Sharon

My response after six hours:

From: Julia Burns
Subject: Pray
Date: July 31, 2014
To: KP, HS, JW, SG PH

Home now.

Thanks,
Julia

Bless you!

Julia

From: Kathy
Subject: Gratitude
Date: July 31, 2014
To: Julia Burns

Good morning, Julia,

Early morning thoughts of you, hoping God did indeed redeem the time and hear our hearts joining yours yesterday as you waited.

I love the way "wait" in the scriptures is often translated as "tarry" and "abide." I am hopeful that Jesus

tarried with you yesterday as you waited on these appointments that are not inherently places of peace.

Thank you for inviting us into your wait, a holy ground.

KP

Yearning

"I'VE GOT THIS BURNING, YEARNING, BURNING FEELING inside me. Ooh deep inside me," l croon, as l head into the lab for a blood draw.

I'll see my provider afterward. And if my labs are good, then l head to the infusion room. What is this burning, yearning feeling inside me? This quest for *Why? Why me? Why now? Why not choose somebody else, God?* My friend told me to pray as if l am a whole, healed beautiful child of God. Healthy, free of disease, and filled with the light of the Holy Spirit, leaping into my future.

"Believe that you will be healed, and embrace it. Then it will happen."

"l was doing that every day already," l replied.

My prayer group encouraged me, reminding me to experience my healing as fulfilled, to know that soon l will be cancer free, playing tennis, doing yoga, painting and creating, living a life filled with health and vitality.

"Do you believe you can be healed?" they said.

"l can't get a read on this. I'm a scientist. It's hard to believe that l will live."

"Do you have someone that does believe? That carries this affirmation for you?"

"Yes. Almost everyone l know."

"That will do."

But l want to know that if believing l will be healed, if God's power is infinite and can lift this plague, then how come it happened in the first place? If l was affirmed as a child of His, living in the light, healthy and whole, my body a temple, then why am l in this waiting room? Why are so many folks standing in this que, stricken with cancer? l wonder. Don't you? How could we not?

Another friend says, "It doesn't matter how or why it happened. The need now is to trust and obey. 'For my thoughts are not your thoughts. My ways are not your ways.'" (Isaiah 55:8–9)

So I patiently wait, sitting in line again, while others get called for their labs. But it's never my turn, and for the third time today, they say, "Doctor Burns, do you have a port?"

"How can you not know that by now?" my typically unflappable husband says to the receptionist. "Don't you know she is a doctor?"

Message: Sometimes the impersonal and bureaucratic approach from hospital personnel can be overwhelming. Be welcoming and loving to them. They have an extremely taxing job—taking care of the sick, and watching patients decline and improve. Try to rise above your irritation and sense of being invisible. Let the light and love of Christ flow from your heart to theirs. He is above and below you, before and behind you, beside you, shining the light which was with Him in the beginning.

The Shave

AND AS THE TREATMENTS CONTINUED, the inevitable happened: my hair melted and had to be shaved.

I waited until after church and communion, because

celebrating the risen Lord on Easter with hair was important. I embraced the vision of weathering treatment with hair, but knew I was not going to make it. In Europe, insurance pays for an ice cap you place on your head during chemo. Since the drugs attack fast-growing cells, freezing the follicles prevents hair loss. But since my treatment was in America, clumps of hair fell into my hands every morning during my shower.

While making plans to shave my head, I caressed my hair as I brushed it for the last time.

"I don't give a rip about losing my hair," I said to the first person who gave me a hat.

Hats and wigs flowed in, some borrowed, some blue.

"I don't. Hair can grow back. What I do care about is having cancer and having this constant pain, and dying."

But when I saw the clumps lying in the drain, tasted hair in my mouth when I was singing "Up From the Grave He Arose," I cared. And I cried.

Tending towards action, I drove myself to Great Cuts for a shave. There were five people ahead of me, and since I had trouble waiting in another line, I called my daughter to see if any of her friends had clippers.

She said, "Yes. Come to Max's."

Owen, whose name means *young warrior*, drove us in my convertible. We put the top down and sang *"Uncle John's Band"* by the Grateful Dead, as my brown tresses waved through the wind one last time.

A lawn chair in the yard held a towel, which I tied around my neck. We started with a mohawk and continued until there was no hair left on my head that could fall in my mouth. My daughter, son, and their young friends sat watching with a spectacular display of courage, telling me how beautiful I looked, how easy this hair cut would be to take care of, and how much they loved it.

Sitting outside by their front stoop, I watched as hair fell at my feet. There was so much it looked like it might belong to someone else.

"The birds will be so happy with this offering," one said. "What a nest they will make."

My daughter's friends were so handsome and healthy it took my breath away. As they held the shears and shaved my head in turns, I blessed their upcoming college graduation, holding hopes for my future, too.

When we finished, a neighbor passed by, walking his little dog on a red leash. He couldn't stop staring. Couldn't turn his head from the spectacle we created. I looked straight back, acknowledging that the public part of this illness had started, the *Oooh, you don't have hair*, and *You look sick*, and *Boy, am I glad I don't have cancer*.

While blessing that stranger and his dog as they walked away, I hoped he was blessing me, too. He had to know. There was only one answer to the question his eyes held when he stared.

Like I said, I don't give a rip about losing my hair. I'm banking on a much bigger miracle.

Message: Let your friends and family love you and take care of you, especially during hard transitions. Believe them when they say you look beautiful bald. Have fun, even during the saddest times. Or just be sad. But try not to be alone.

Julia, Come Out

BEAR WITH ME, PLEASE, while I have a hitch in my faith.

While pondering healing and the possibility of altering my fate by what I think and believe, I project an image of myself holding my granddaughter, rocking her in the chair where I nursed my children. As I fill a grape jelly glass adorned with Wiley Coyote, one that I drank from as a child, I envision a grandson sitting beside me, lifting it to his lips. And then, as clearly as in a movie, I see my husband casting a line in the New Hope Creek, giving fishing lessons as my grandchildren clamor, begging for a try.

Jesus' voice echoes throughout the cancer center: "Lazarus, come out."

Come out, indeed. I'm trying to come.

Reverberations of this poignant story—Christ raising his friend Lazarus from the dead—upend my thinking and faith, reminding me that Christ is the great healer.

"Unbind her and let her go. I say this for the sake of the crowd standing there so that they may believe that you sent me."

Jesus knew that He did not need to implore the Father, because His Father always listens and already knows. And I know that, too. Nonetheless, I do beseech Him for strength, courage, renewed health, and tolerance for long waits in the waiting room. He has already heard and answered my prayer, my story written before time began. Yet I am praying repetitively, hoping the script can be altered by these petitions.

I'm sure you remember that Lazarus did come out, just as Jesus expected. And yet Jesus wept in his sadness at their unbelief.

53

Message: Jesus holds you in his hands every moment, every day. When you feel the most abandoned, He is closest. Never doubt how much He loves you and how much He is trying to heal you. When you can't remember or feel this, ask others to remind you.

Patch of Blue

"IT'S A GRAY DAY," an old Scottish cobbler once said.

"Yes, but didn't ya see the patch of blue?"

But as the patch of blue disappeared, I lost my balance. A dear friend had a cardiac episode on the tennis court. A week of tests was bringing bad news. More diagnostic evaluations were scheduled for both of us, and I grieved because I couldn't help, couldn't be with her children at this critical time. I could only lie on the sofa and ponder life—mine and hers.

The inflammation was shrinking in size and density, yet still I feared the mammogram. How was I going to put my thick, inflamed, painful breast between two pieces of plastic and let them pull the trigger to squeeze and pinch? Anger and indignation grew, and I became the source of my suffering.

My neighbor had a stroke and died two days after. Walking toward the church for her funeral, I passed a woman screaming on her cell phone. She was obnoxious and stressed, angry and out of control.

I thought, *Why is this woman so outraged? Surely she should be the sick one, not me.* I wished to pass this cancer on, slip a few fingers under my right breast and lift this painful growth so rudely inserted, and give it away.

Envying my neighbor, her sudden departure, I lamented. She had shared a chocolate malt with her husband just hours before the stroke. Fifty years of marriage, and they were still drinking malted milkshakes together, just like they had in high school.

I wondered if I would be married another year.

"Blessed are they that mourn, for they shall be comforted," Jesus said to the crowd gathered by the sea of Galilee, in the Sermon on the Mount. Not, *Blessed are the angry, and those holding judgments.*

Job's friends wondered at his misery, urged him to curse God so he could be released.

"You have the power to free yourself from your infirmities," they told him.

But Job stood fast in his devotion, never forsaking the Creator, who gave him life.

I want to be like Job, and I am telling you of my bitter anger so you will see my humanity.

Lifting the plea, "Not me, Lord. Not this," I catch myself and change the refrain to, "Thank you, Lord. Thank you for this moment, this peace that passes understanding, this suffering, this freedom from fear."

Thank you, Lord, for the little patch of blue shining so strongly out of the gray.

Message: It is only human to resent and refuse your diagnosis and pain. The Lord understands and forgives us. There will be days when you want to "pass this cup," and days when you feel certain all is going well. It feels like surfing—up and down, inside and out.

Learn to ride the waves, and your trip will be more enjoyable. Release and let go. Trust God.

Suffering

"I WON'T BE THIS PERSON, OR HAVE THIS CANCER. My life will not be shattered by this monster that stings like a scorpion and robs my energy so I can barely load the washing machine. Leaves me lying on the sofa, examining the day's activities and coming up short."

Last week, I was questioning. But in the end, I will acquiesce once more. I will sit and meditate on pain and suffering, mine and others'. I will sit and pray for equanimity, releasing the judgments that light a fire in my belly and hurt no one but me. Remembering the first noble truth, that life is suffering, I am struck by how easy it is to forget, especially when you need it most.

A deep exhalation relaxes my chest.

Where there is suffering, there will be happiness, and liberation comes through my intention not to grasp at it. If I let joy find me, there it will be:

I join my husband for coffee, because he stays home now instead of rushing off to work. Nightly, I listen to my daughter read Psalm 91. I praise the Great Physician as a nurse infuses the Cytoxan. I pray that my healthy cells will be protected. And I receive Snapchats from my children making crazy faces. Paddington, my dog, snuggles beside me when I am too weary to move. Email inquiries from my blog subscribers praise my strength. And I walk through my gardens when I can't walk down the street. Happiness.

In order to live, I must cast aside judgments and fears of test results. My life is sweet, and yes, made sweeter by this strange malady. Family gathers closer, and friends read the Bible in concert, blessing and sending me vibrations of love and light with earnest petitions for wholeness. Tidings of great joy come without ceasing.

> **Message:** Often, when you feel the angriest is when you are about to turn from fear and judgment and slide into joy and hope. You remember all your blessings, and maybe even write them down in your journal. Remind yourself, especially when the darkness envelops you, that you are strong, loved, and cared for.

Darkness

THEN THE PITY PARTY BEGAN. The medicine they gave me to increase bone growth made me sicker than chemotherapy. Lying on the sofa for days with what I thought was the flu, I moaned. Too sick to move, to achy to eat, I thought, *If I feel this bad, could it mean more metastasis?*

They tell me this bone density infusion decreases bone metastasis. But how do you know what to do when the cancer is so aggressive and the research data is new? If I say, *"No, I don't want this. It makes me too sick,"* they'll talk me into it with statistics about recurrence. And as shame and fear strip you, you say, "Where does God's grace and my faith intersect?" and "Will it be enough to see me through?"

I couldn't wait to go to my prayer group. And as they lifted me, the cloud departed. After giving thanks for the hospital and the doctors and the cutting-edge treatment, I thanked the Great Physician for family and friends that pray daily, not for survival, but for thriving health. They hold me when I stumble, and pray for me when I can't pray for myself.

Message: It is not unusual for doctors to minimize or forget the side effects of the treatments they recommend. Remember, you can do your own research and accept or refuse treatments based on your body's response. You are the chairman of your treatment team.

Rip Tides

ONE DAY AT THE BEACH, THE SUFFERING NEARLY ENDED. While swimming in the ocean, I watched an enormous black cloud roll over from the sound side, with ominous thunder, but no lightening. I looked down and saw a young girl being pulled deep into the ocean, her bright yellow boogie board flying away from her, and washing up on shore. Her young friend swam after her, but came back crying. The mom looked up, swam out, and encouraged her daughter to tread water and not to be afraid. And just as fast as the undertow brought the girl out, the mother brought her back in. Soon, the two girls were digging in the sand, building sand castles and laughing together.

And that's when that rip took me. I had waded out to

greet them, being careful not to go in over my knees. But I wasn't careful enough, because the bottom dropped out and I was in up to my chin. Knowing how to swim in a riptide, I started the sidestroke, parallel to shore. But I gained no ground.

Further out and barely touching, I felt foolish because earlier I had pointed out those perpendicular waves to my husband. The calmer surface waters hiding a deeper turbulence. We agreed that if I was to swim after he left the beach, I should be careful.

My husband is going to kill me if I die in this ocean after all we've done this year to save my life.

Then the same little girl who had been carried out, saw me jumping, waving, and yelling, and told her mom, who swam out and calmly directed me to swim in the other direction, which I did. I rolled closer to shore, and she reached out and grabbed my hand.

I wonder if God took me to the brink of drowning to convince me of a new way of seeing my physical healing. The ocean's smooth surface covered a mighty riptide rolling out and upside down, taking me to the brink of destruction, and then peacefully setting me on shore. Perhaps He's watching to see how I do things now that I have another chance for living.

"Faith is believing in what we do not see, and the reward for this kind of faith is to see what we believe," St. Augustine said.

Stand on the beach and watch keenly for ripples in the tides of your life. Walk boldly into the most dangerous riptides, safely buoyed by the Holy Spirit. Believe in the power of Christ to guide as you are dragged into the deep and over your head. Believe in the unseen manifesting in the seen. This faith I choose.

Message: Choose to see what you believe, and to believe what you see. Imagine getting stronger and healthier every day. Surround yourself with positive people who believe this, too. When the riptide carries you out and under, swim along the shore and watch yourself wash up to the beach, safe and secure.

New Promises

THREE SHOOTING STARS AND THE SUN'S FINGERS LIT THE DAY as a song rang out.

> *Here comes the sun,*
> *do, dun, do, do.*
> *Here comes the sun,*
> *and I say*
> *It's all right.*
> —The Beatles

Ann

A FRIEND VISITED DURING MY TREATMENT, and we were standing near a train track by my azaleas when this song came. She was a dear, dear friend. One who believed in my writing from the beginning.

I know when I hear that melancholy sound
that want slides in to capture it.
Trap it in a mason jar and
screw the lid on tight,
letting it thrash around that transparent glass,
whooing in closed-in spaces.
What gets triggered when the whistle blows
and sings back in that same
mournful, wistful tune?
Is it ever going to be yesterday again?
That moment you have when the
train clamors by and
you stand with your friend
in a garden near the trestle, white azaleas
soaring so high above your heads.
What crashes away while you stand there,
bathed in silver decrescendos of fragrance,
and blowing?
And how come it never seems to
carry you away completely?

Persistence

BOREDOM AND COTTONMOUTH: my main problems are hard to admit. Also, I can't spell anymore. I'm embarrassed because I've read about terrible side effects—cardiomyopathy, renal failure, liver damage, peripheral neuropathy, nausea, vomiting, infections, and rash. And I have the audacity to complain about boredom and cottonmouth.

I was sure I'd regret this. My silly whining, when I could have life-threatening problems. And sure enough, regret seized me yesterday when my left leg disappeared and was dragging so that I could barely finish my walk.

"You weren't grateful, and now look," I told myself.

Luckily, the numbness left the next day. But the boredom, the *Wow, this is taking a long time*, remained.

When the chemotherapy is over, I have a modified radical mastectomy scheduled. And after that, six weeks of radiation. After all the traditional treatment, there is a clinical trial, a multi-modal research protocol my oncologist wants me to enroll in. I hope I get randomized into an active drug. Praying on my cushion, I banish thoughts of death that creep in.

"Trust God, no matter how dark the day may seem."

And I do. I am persistent, if not perfect.

Message: Persistent, not perfect, is what God calls us to be. It is not easy to fall on his grace and mercy when we are facing long months of treatment. How do we relinquish control when our future is so uncertain? It is only with great intention and support. Lean on God, ask your prayer partners to help you surrender, and let them know when you falter.

Strike Three

WHEN THEY TOLD ME MY PROGNOSIS and diagnosis—sort of in that order—I didn't believe them. Breast cancer was never in my life plan. Certainly not a breast cancer with such a low survival rate. I was counting on Hong Kong and India. I also wanted to bike in Sicily.

You've got the wrong breast, my mind screamed, doubting the red-headed practitioner whose face went white when she touched my breast.

She promised to pray for me. I didn't want her prayers. I wanted her to shut up and stop talking about multi-disciplinary teams and chemotherapy starting next week.

Painting, gardening, and cooking hold no interest now. I'm too tired. But I still love seeing patients, and writing, and watching movies. I also like reading and playing Trivial Pursuit. I like sitting down. I'm good at sitting down. Whoever thought my biggest problem would be *How to be sick for ten months?*

I don't know how to slow down and do nothing while my body heals and my immune system kickstarts this fight for life, rejecting this cancer. Believing in wholeness and not the NIH statistics on survival, I'd say we're doing something amazing. Our cumulative efforts have created a winning team.

In a vision, I see myself standing on home plate, at bat, with the bases full. After pounding the ball over the fence, I round the diamond and slide into home, scoring the winning run. The crowd is cheering wildly.

Up to bat every Wednesday, Taxol is rounding the bases, too, polymerizing microtubules, immobilizing mutant growths. What can I fear when I hear the crowd roar? So many cheerleaders encouraging me, so how can I die? Instead, I celebrate the power that is bringing us together in this game of healing. Strike three, inflammatory breast cancer. You're out!

Message: Give yourself the luxury of fantasizing. Imagine your cancer cells melting in a furnace, or being eaten by Pacman. Don't limit the extent of your creativity as you exterminate your mutant cells and activate your healthy ones. Envision your future without cancer.

I Hear Death Knocking

"With long life will I satisfy her
and show her my salvation."

—Psalm 91:16

LONG LIFE—THAT'S THE PROMISE I HEAR. The psalmist David wrote a love song to God, declaring thanks for restitution and protection. Even after he sinned with another man's wife, murdered her husband, gave way to an awful malady, and was hunted down like an animal, he praised God, begging not to be forgotten.

Typically, I sing praises of gratitude also. But recently, there has been more lamenting. And King David assures me that lamenting is also noble.

Return to your rest, O my soul, for the Lord
has dealt bountifully with you. For you have
rescued my soul from death, my eyes from
tears, and my feet from stumbling. I shall walk
before the Lord in the land of the living.
—Psalm 116.

The chemo was extended from twelve weeks to sixteen, and it's hard. I find myself weeping in bed after my husband has gone to work, reading Thich Nhat Hanh's *No Fear, No Death*. I row my boat over the pages of eternity. "The flame in the match is always there, although it is not manifest until we strike it. When we strike the match and light the candle, blowing out the match, is the flame still manifest in the match?"

"Yes!" I yell from my bed, my soul ascending over my body.

Surely death is more like a snake shedding its skin and slithering off to parts unknown, than a mere snake skin lying lifeless and abandoned without a journey.

In this misery, I put down Tich Nhat Hahn and look at photo albums Momma created with love—a baby in a smocked dress, a middle schooler in a homemade orange striped jumper, a college student sitting at a football game, cheering. Am I this person or that other? Is the one who types and posts, paints and heals the same girl that won the third-grade spelling bee, but now can't spell *brilliant*? Is that girl who placed second in the state audition contest with a Mozart concerto the same one that can barely play hymns today? Who will my daughter be when I pass away, if not mine?

Once born, does the trajectory of life continue throughout eternity, interrupted by the twists and turns of time, until
each piece separates before coming back together to create a
unified whole? I realize that God knows when I will shed this
skin for parts unknown. He knows I do not. But what I do
know is that I will never die. I will be manifest or non-mani-
fest like the flame in the match, but will never cease to exist. I
am with and not with, forever.

> **Message:** There will be times when death and
> thoughts of death chase you. This is
> normal and cannot be avoided. When
> your doctors tell you that your disease
> is life-threatening, you are going to be
> fearful. When these thoughts invade your
> thinking, don't try to chase them away. Sit
> with them. God has promised eternity to
> those who believe in Him. You are life. As
> it was in the beginning, it is now, and shall
> be forever.

Side Effects

I HAVE NO BAD NEWS. Truly, I don't. It's just that I don't
feel like myself. As I near the end of twenty-four weeks of
infusions, I am different, more like a seventy-five-year-old
woman, dulled from this extended process of toxic cleansing.
I drop things. I forget. I'm uninterested. I'm not depressed,
but I am flat.

I'm having an art show in a café this month because
I want to do something concrete to combat this malaise.

What are They So Mad About? is a show featuring five artists whose childhood trauma informs their art—Tyler Perry, Oprah Winfrey, Maya Angelou, Virginia Woolf, and Elizabeth Barrett Browning. All were emotionally, physically, or sexually abused in childhood, and used their life scripts to inspire originality. I am proud to have known each one through creating their portraits.

Message: Even when you don't feel like it, plan something concrete to redeem your time. Make a cake, plan a meal for your family, sing, play an instrument, paint, or garden. If you can't garden, take a small patch in your yard and hire a gardener to execute your ideas. Plant that small vegetable garden you've been dreaming about. Don't give in to the lethargy. Pace yourself. You are the best one to measure when to be active and when to rest.

From: Kathy
Subject: Blog
Date: August 18, 2014
To: Julia Burns

Hi, Julia,

I read your blog—very interesting and not off-putting; you've made faith claims in previous blogs, so it's not like people would be shocked that you follow Jesus.

What I liked about your comments is that you gave a nice summary for anyone who would want to further investigate the idea of spiritual healing. Also, you simply dispel the idea that poor health is God's desire to punish or correct or get your attention.

Not that he won't use any negative experience for our good—because obviously he had done so with you, and me, and countless others I know…but that he is not the creator of it.

I think God does use people in position of influence to press His Kingdom further into the darkness, even the medical establishment!

KP

Outrage

THIS CHAPTER IS ABOUT ANGER. Anger at acquaintances who callously imply that *Either way, you'll be fine. God will take care of you.*

Of course, I know that God will take care of me, that His will be done, that life on this planet is transitory. That doesn't mean I'm ready for the transit. I know this is a fallen world and that everyone exits. But I really, really want to survive. I want to live to be mother at my children's weddings. Live to hold my grandchildren. Live to experience a movie night with my daughter. Live, just live.

The arrogance and insensitivity of someone in good health, with no threat of death snatching them, to lean over and announce my good fortune, my luck at being so well taken care of. Reassurances that *Either way, I'll be fine,* bring me up short and make me silent. What can I say but, "I know that." But I don't want to live "either way." I want to live this way, this earthly way. I want more time with family and friends, more time to practice medicine, to pray, paint, and write. I want those renegade cells growing rampantly in my body to cease and desist, to give way to health, to balance each other and kill the cancer. I want the cells in my body to come under the direction of Christ. I want people that aren't dying to stop telling me how good I look, how fine I am, how great my journey will become. I'm not ready for this lecture on Death 101.

How about somebody with good health, without cancer, looks me in the eye and says, *"I'm sorry this happened. I'd trade places with you if I could. I'll die in your place if you want to live."* Sound familiar? It does to me. Jesus did that long ago, and he's doing it every day, for all of us. Take a lesson from a psychiatrist. Don't tell a person in the beginning stages of fighting a life-threatening disease that it will be fine, either way. Because it won't.

Message: Many well-meaning people will say the most insensitive things. Some will make you mad. Some will bring you up short and just make you feel sorry for someone who could be so ridiculously insensitive. Get ready. It is going to happen. If it makes you angry, go with it. Think of a way to tell them if you want. But remember, you are the most important person in the equation. Do what feels right to you. Ignoring the information is fine also.

The Fight

"Being left alone by Satan is not evidence of being blessed."

This quote is one of my favorites these days, making me thankful for this adversity.

At first, it scared me when my prayer group reminded me that we are all engaged in a spiritual war, and that I had been selected as a powerful foe, that God would create something beautiful, wise, kind, and compassionate through this dreadful process. They reminded me of Paul's letter to the Ephesians: "Our fight is not against flesh and blood, but against principalities, against powers, against the rulers of darkness of this world." (Ephesians 6:12)

The Message translates it this way:

> And that about wraps it up. God is strong, and he wants you strong. So take everything the Master has set out for you, well-made weapons of the best materials. And put them to use so you will be able to stand up to everything the Devil throws your way. This is no afternoon athletic contest that we'll walk away from and forget about in a couple of hours. This is for keeps, a life-or-death fight to the finish against the Devil and all his angels. Be prepared. You're up against far more than you can handle on your own. Take all the help you can get, every weapon God has issued, so that when it's all over, you'll still be on your feet. Truth, righteousness, peace, faith, and salvation are more than words. Learn how to apply them. You'll need them throughout your life. God's Word is an indispensable weapon. In the same way, prayer is essential in this ongoing warfare. Pray hard and long. Pray for your brothers and sisters. Keep your eyes open. Keep each other's spirits up so that no one falls behind or drops out. (Ephesians 6:10–20)

Each morning, outfitting myself with the armor of God, I put on the helmet of salvation, gird my waist with truth, and fastened the breastplate of righteousness. Can you see those beautiful gemstones gleaming—pink, aqua, yellow, and sky blue? After putting on the red shoes of peace, I walk forward without fear. Emboldened by scripture and the sword of light, I place white roses over my chest, creating a shield of faith. I walk through the day with this protection, knowing that serving others and worshiping God is all that is required.

"To be left alone by Satan is to be labeled ineffective."

Never wanting to be ineffective, 1 prepare for battle, repelling the roaring wolf who prowls about, seeking to destroy me, my family, and my friends, opening myself to love.

Message: Surely it is hard to think of the devil prowling around after us. We want to walk in the light of Christ and leave darkness behind. But the Bible shows us time and again that we live in a fallen world, and that we have to fight the enemy. Whether our attacks come as disease, idolatry, or laziness, they await us. I remember when I had a vision that God had not given me cancer. That as polluters and poor guardians of the earth, we had created so much toxicity in our food, air, water, and earth that we had given God cancer. He gave us the garden of Eden, and we let that slip through our fingers out of greed and ignorance. Now these toxins are making us sick.

Unbreakable

"UNBREAKABLE! I'M ALIVE, DAMMIT. It's a miracle. Unbreakable! I'm alive, dammit. This female is strong as hell," I sing, in the shower, repelling the forces of death and destruction that threaten to level me.

In the process of searching for explanations, 1 find

comfort in the promise that Jesus set my healing in scripture before I ever got sick. I look up the story of the hemorrhaging woman who crawled through the crowd, seeking to touch Jesus' robe and be made whole. Her story brings peace and reinforces my efforts to turn away from sickness and into health. I crawl with her to my Savior, hand extended to brush the miracle of that robe.

"Heal me, too," I cry, with assuredness that I sometimes don't feel.

Then I remember, I'm unbreakable and alive, dammit.

And on Tuesday, my physical exam, labs, and MRI confirm this. It's a miracle.

> **Message:** Choose a healing miracle story from the Bible and make yourself that character. Imagine yourself being lowered through the roof for Jesus' blessing, or having your bleeding stop after twelve years, at the exact moment when you touch Jesus' robe. Envision Jesus touching you, and you being made whole. It happened many times in the New Testament, feeding the five thousand, changing water into wine. It can happen to you as well. Expect it. Believe it.

Unilateral or Bi?

"WHAT'S THE MATTER? Why didn't they take your breasts?"

"You wouldn't let them take your boobs? They could have whacked mine off, no problem."

"That's not the protocol for IBC," I whisper. "Trust me, this is one show I'm not running, even if I am a doctor. Doing the mastectomy *after* chemotherapy has increased the survival rate from approximately zero to twenty-five percent."

I'm in group therapy on Wednesdays, and the leaders encourage attention to outrage. One example of outrage is road rage. Getting angry with a stranger who cuts you off is more about you than them. It is most often because we are mad about something else. Outrage is a clue to anger.

And yes, I'm angry—about having cancer, about the inconvenience of organizing my life around hospital visits, about my family's fear of my death, and how it's breaking my daughter. I am exhausted by it. Tired of medicines that are diminishing me. I'm worn out and irritable.

My meltdown about *God loves you either way* is a reflection of how afraid I am. Not of dying, exactly. More of wasting away and missing everything. I'm looking forward to living with the Trinity. I just don't want to leave my family and this earth to do it. So I'm seeking something in between the two.

This rage drives my recovery as I muster defenses and keep on going—taking walks, lifting weights, doing Pilates, painting, writing, working, and believing. This anger fuels my life force and creates healing.

Message: It is OK to be angry and to let that feeling lift you out of complacency and into the fight for your life. Let your feelings settle around you, and ask God what he wants out of those feelings. Ask him how to manage the anger and use it to your advantage. Jesus got angry when the temple was being violated. You can have a multitude of feelings—anger, joy, and gratitude are some.

How Much Longer?

MY SIX-YEAR OLD COUSIN BECAME RESTLESS in church on Sunday.

"How much longer?" he said, using his big boy voice.

It was a reasonable question, but his parents ignored him.

"How much longer?" he repeated, a bit louder. "I'm asking a simple question."

They were sitting in front, so his father turned to him and whispered, "Ten more minutes."

"What?" The decibel level rose slightly once more. "What did you say?"

And then it was full tantrum time, ten minutes being an eternity. He started scuffling and kicking his feet until he accidently kicked his mother. It was the day before first grade, and I'm sure that this young boy knew the freedom he loved and cherished was over, even as his father led him out of the sanctuary.

And I wanted to stand up and kick my feet, too, wave my arms, beat my chest, and shout, "How much longer?"

Life-and-death questions demand answers. At least half of the congregation must have a similar dilemma. I notice my breathlessness as I walk to communion, wondering if God's plan for how much longer will ever match mine.

If we were all honest, if we weren't so well-behaved and

restrained, we might kick and yell, *"I asked a simple question, and I want an answer!"*

Surely God prefers the honesty of my little cousin to the well-behaved complacency of the congregation.

"I turned to the Lord God and pleaded with him in prayer and petition, in fasting and in sackcloth and ashes." (Daniel 9:3) Isn't that what Jesus did in the garden, on the night before he died, when he moaned, "Abba, Father, everything is possible for you. Take this cup from me. Yet not what I will, but what you will." (Mark 14:36)

I bet he even raised his voice and stomped in exasperation and disbelief at the apostles' betrayal when he walked back to find them asleep. Much like my cousin, little Samuel, did when asked to sit too long, either in church or school. Very much like the way I felt when the nurse practitioner congratulated me on completing my chemotherapy, and then the oncologist walked in and added four more treatments.

"Your name will no longer be Jacob, but Israel, because you have struggled with God and with men and have overcome." (Genesis 32:28)

Change my name to Israel, Lord. And Samuel's, too. Let us rise, growing stronger every day. Bend our wills to your wisdom as we forsake ourselves.

Message: We will stand up and wrestle with God. Another story about righteous indignation. How much longer, Lord, and how can I use my outrage to glorify you? The struggle is real, and the fight long. He honors us when we show up and ask questions.

Will the Real Healer Please Stand Up?

SAYING GOODBYE TO MY PATIENTS brought sadness and tears, but a two-month sabbatical was necessary to prepare for and recover from surgery. Our time together and the work we do is meaningful. They will have a hard time replacing me. They are not replaceable.

Residency taught me that I was the healer—my patients were not to take care of me; I was to care for them. But I have never found this to be true, as healing is always in relationship—more of a circle than a straight line.

Metamorphosis—theirs and mine—happens when patients commit to regular appointments. Even when I was being kicked at and spit on by an adolescent during a hold in the timeout room of the residential treatment facility, I knew profound communication was taking place. Honored to be in the conversation, I believed my patients' declarations—verbal and nonverbal—and listened to every message.

Messages from my patients were supportive, even as I announced my illness. They demonstrated great faith in my recovery, and many presents appeared—an Easter cake, wigs, books, and movies. They believed in my ability to take care of them, even as my fingers and feet went numb and my memory diminished. Applauding my bald head as it began to fuzz, commenting on my color and stamina, always counting on my return to work after surgery, they affirmed how much they needed me. And each patient was added to the list of things for which I had to live.

When I got up on Mondays and descended the stairs to my basement office, I was transformed from sick to well, from patient to doctor. I became a trusted confidante whose ability to listen, ask questions, and pray for healing made a difference. I don't care how many lectures I got in residency about patients not taking care of their doctors. I don't believe it, because it isn't true.

Message: Deciding whether to continue to work or to take a sabbatical is not easy. It requires deliberation, and perhaps, consulting others—family, physicians, co-workers, and mentors. If your work is taxing physically, it may be best to take a break. If your work inspires you and distracts you from your illness, working could be helpful. Perhaps part-time work is available. Do your own analysis. You can always re-assess and change if your decision doesn't work out.

Will I still be Beautiful?

I'M AT THE BEACH, PREPARING mentally and physically for this modified, radical resection that is going to alter my life and appearance, possibly saving me at the same time. Later that day, I am swimming in the ocean when I feel eyes watching.

Good. I'm glad someone sees me swimming, I thought, feeling safer under another's gaze.

How will I navigate without breasts in a breast-centric society? Initially, I was so sure that I wanted a bilateral. My mother got breast cancer for the second time at age eighty-four, and her post-op recovery was difficult. So when they asked, I said, "Yes, take both."

But now, I'm wavering. And as I listen to my surgeon talk about losing nodes with the resection on the healthy left side, doubts crowd in. His brusque, loud, and urgent insistence that a "bilateral is best. What about that can I not understand?" did not help in the discernment. My husband's admonition that taking two was twice as invasive as one stuck deep in the recesses of my brain. I was confused and conflicted. Mostly, I wanted to be healthy and keep both breasts.

"You'll have to have a tummy tuck so they can use the fat to make your boobs."

"You're too young, too beautiful not to have reconstruction, Julia."

"Who's doing the remake?"

And on go the questions about reconstruction, until I start doubting that flat is beautiful, and start to change my mind.

"Why do girls have those things on their chest?" a kindergartener says to his grandfather.

"Oh, those are breasts, and they are for feeding babies."

"What happens after the baby finishes eating? Are they just for decoration?"

His grandfather roared, repeating this conversation to anyone who would listen.

I think back to his joke and wonder, *What will life be like without my decorations?*

As I observed the man on the beach watching me jump and slide in the surf, I wondered if anyone would look at me that way after surgery.

This chapter is dedicated to the many brave women who have slept while surgeons—mostly male—drew a line around their breasts, and cut and sawed away. Women who, in this sacrifice, hoped they would live longer. Isn't that all we hoped for when we made this decision—unilateral or bilateral? And it's what our families hoped for also.

Message: Determining between a unilateral or bilateral is another challenging choice. Just as I was discerning, research was beginning to show that complications from a bilateral may make a unilateral safer. But if you choose a unilateral, then you have to wear a prosthesis to be balanced. I didn't feel like I wanted to wear a prosthesis every day. I couldn't get reconstruction because my cancer was too aggressive. Also, most of my friends had more complications from their reconstruction than their mastectomy, and I didn't want that.

My surgeon was rude. I had no one to help me decipher the literature. This uncertainty about the outcome led me to feel alone and unsure about the process. Seek out providers who care about helping you decide.

Diaries

SITTING ON THE PORCH AT THE BEACH, I was drinking coffee when an influx of yellow butterflies danced across the marsh.

"There go ten, eleven, twelve, thirteen...thirty-one...fifty...sixty-one...eighty-three...one hundred four," I chanted as they continued coming.

Chill and wind pierced me, so I decided to go inside, knowing that after I left, the dance would continue.

I looked them up on the computer and found their name: yellow diaries. Lovely butterflies keeping secrets as they flit and float over the marsh in song, writing poems and stories with their wings. We are kindred spirits.

Hundreds of tiny yellow fliers buoyant above the grass, float from dock to dock, not stopping to graze as they search for home. And this migration parallels my journey from sickness to wholeness as cancer takes me to a place of never going back, never starting at the beginning again.

"Life will never be the way it was before," my daughter says.

"Ah, but isn't it better?" I reply, in humble recognition that God has graced us with an illness that could have brought us to our knees, but instead has increased our spirit and faith.

He will never leave me, and just like my daughter, He is filled with steadfast love.

Looking for signs of my outcome, I ponder the diaries. Do they represent miracles of healing, or the transformation to spirit? Do they foretell the songs I have left to write and sing, or portend blossoming on the other side? Some days, I am sure it is one, and then I am convinced of the other.

Living in the confidence that my work here is not complete, I grasp God's hand in the knowledge that He will heal me spiritually, always; and physically, if possible.

As hundreds of diaries flit past my view, lighting on the marsh grass in neon yellow, they sing a secret song of promise, and I sit humbly and believe.

> **Message:** You may look for omens in nature that support your path to healing. Sitting outside and immersing yourself in nature rejuvenates you, calms your nervous system, and boosts your immune system. Spend time outside absorbing the sun's rays, resting in the glory of creation.

Anger

MY DAUGHTER, WILTON, AND I went to speak with my psychiatrist, therapist, and supervisor about anger. Even though every Wednesday, she halted her research in marine biology (the flow cytometer ceasing its phytoplankton counts) to sit by me in the infusion room, and even though she was devoted to me and these treatments, she was angry.

"Mom, get up and get your own glass of water. I saw you do it yesterday. I'm not waiting on you."

Turns out, it's not unusual for children to be mad at their parents when they threaten to die. Not unusual, but painful.

I turned to my prayer group, in tears: "I don't know how I'm going to leave my daughter. I can wrap my head around leaving the boys and my husband. They will be fine. But I don't see my daughter having children without me. I can't do this."

My prayer group reminded me that God would parent my children better than I ever could. Perhaps my doubts fueled her fury, because underneath the love and considerate moments was another volatile emotion—one neither of us knew how to handle.

"So tell us how you feel about your mother's cancer," my therapist said to her.

The answers came tumbling out: "I don't want you to die. I can't forgive this horrible thing that's growing inside. I'm so mad this is happening to us. It's not fair. When you talk about Jesus healing you, it makes me feel like what I do doesn't count."

I looked at her and said, "If you don't get over this, it's going to destroy us. You have to believe that our love is larger than this disease. When your heart is too small for the problem, it must expand. It must evolve. God's great love is more than sufficient. My love for you is enough. I would never do this on purpose. You have to believe me."

She's so young. I witnessed her struggle to expand, to conquer this anger that made her do the opposite of what her heart willed as she fussed at me for my weakness.

Two weeks before I knew about the infection that turned out to be cancer, we met for lunch. Sitting in my car, we ate egg salad sandwiches. The filling in Wilton's sandwich dripped down her shirt, much like it did when she was younger, reminding me of the lifelong love we shared for each other and egg salad sandwiches. Tears came to my eyes, and before I knew it, I was weeping.

"What? What's wrong? Why are you crying, Mom?" she said, as the tears were sliding down her face, too.

"Nothing. Just love. I promise," I replied, as our hearts filled with passion.

I visualized a waterfall coming out of my chest, enveloping and bathing us.

Somehow, in this unspoken communication, it seemed as though we discerned my dark illness, which loomed in the future.

Together. Always together.

Recalling this moment of intense revelation later, when the doctors were pronouncing death, we cried again.

After all the test results were in, my husband and I called my middle son, Owen, and my daughter, and asked them to come to the house.

She ran in. "Mom, what's wrong? We both prayed the whole way here that the dog had been run over, or something else terrible, because we knew it was bad news. You've never called us home at the same time. What did your tests show?"

Then her father told them the news, holding back some of the details, particularly the ones about liver metastasis and keeping me comfortable. Now she is fearful, unable to process what we both felt that moment when she spilled egg salad on her shirt and we burst into tears—tenderness wedged between panic. I sit, watching helplessly as she weeps, silently imploring her to pardon this reality that neither she nor I can completely comprehend.

Message: You may experience anger from some of your family members, or even close friends. This is normal and requires expression. It is doubtful that it will just go away. People that love you and are close, especially your children, may feel scared about living without you. They may blame themselves for the illness, and cover that up by blaming you. If you have a therapist, you might want to consult them. If not, most cancer treatment programs offer counseling with a social worker, in group or individual settings. Take advantage of this. Let your family and friends be honest about their feelings regarding your illness and possible death. Be honest about yours as well.

Surgery

SURGERY AND PAIN CREATE SILENCE. Thus, having nothing to say, I say nothing. I can hardly stand. This agony is excruciating.

I'd be a Liar if I said I Did

ONE OF MY HUSBAND'S LEAST FAVORITE Southern sayings occurs when you ride for miles, only to stop and seek directions from the owner of a gas station.

"Do you know where Lewis Crossroads is? We're hopelessly lost."

"Suuuuurrrreee don't. I'd be a liar if I said I did."

Back he comes to the car, fuming. "Why do they say sure if they mean don't?"

And like most natives, I don't have an answer, never having noticed this odd turn of phrase I'd grown up with. But I'd be a liar if I said that the reason I haven't blogged lately is that I've been busy. I'd be a liar if I said that the last two months have been delightful and not full of disappointment and pain.

It started post-op, in the ambulatory care center, when a vein on my left side bled for hours and they couldn't find a doctor. That vein tore and continued to leak until my pulse quickened and my blood pressure dropped. We were told it was difficult to get doctors for patients in ambulatory care.

"What in the world were you doing there in the first place?" my friends said to me.

I didn't have an answer, and I'd be a liar if I said I did.

They urge you to eat after your surgery so they can document intake and output and send you home. As my pressure dropped, I got nauseous. Getting sicker, I vomited the green beans I knew I shouldn't have eaten. The nurse said that the monitor beeping a lower and lower blood pressure was "probably not correct," but still I couldn't have any pain medicine, "just in case it was right."

Finally, my sister said, "You've been saying the doctor was on the way for four hours. What is going on?"

At about 9:15 p.m., after I called my oncologist at home, the oncology fellow came, placed a pressure dressing over the vein, drew blood, and hung a bag of saline. After that infusion, I was blessed with higher blood pressure, and allowed pain medicine. Imagine the torment of no pain medicine for hours after a bilateral mastectomy.

I'd be a liar if I said I didn't have to work hard at forgiving that nurse, even as my oncologist called and asked for my vital signs. The nurse refused her any information, based on HIPPA, and she left me alone to vomit again. Not even the orderly would come into the room as the situation deteriorated. I thought I was dying.

They sent me home the next day despite a blood pressure that was still precariously low. A nurse practitioner came in to teach the importance of exercises, and gave me a handout.

Processing information or standing up was impossible because my blood pressure was still so low. The roar in my head was all I could hear. I didn't do those exercises the first day, and I'd be a liar if I said I did. Every time I stood and tried to raise my arm, the room dipped and swayed.

That vein tearing and bleeding caused an accumulation on my left, "good" side. My surgeon wanted to suction out the blood so the swelling would go down and the pain would abate. I'd be a liar if I said it did, because a few days later, I got a raging infection and antibiotics were prescribed.

The swelling reminds you of a tooth ache, only much bigger, across your whole chest and under your arms, with relentless throbbing.

I stayed on that antibiotic for two and a half weeks, getting worse day after day, until finally the infection responded. I can break into a cold sweat now, years later, just thinking about it. Guess that's why I stopped writing. I didn't know what to say that wasn't awful.

Our anniversary occurred during this time, and my husband bought me a card that said, "I honestly believe that we are two of the luckiest people on earth." Inside it read, "We've got a great life."

At first, it made me angry. I wanted to say, *"You might be lucky. But I'm not so sure about me."*

Then I started thinking about all my blessings: A surgeon who did a fabulous job and can't help the spasm of a tiny vein bleeding and causing trouble; my oncologist, who, when I told her I'd found inflammatory breast cancer on the Internet which sounded like my symptoms, had replied, "Why don't you come in tomorrow at eight a.m."; my husband, who waited on me and did everything he could to ease my suffering; my daughter, who came to every chemo and lay in the bed with me afterward, pressing on my head, hands, feet or whatever hurt; Owen, who made a video singing to my good health; Andrew, who was so worried that he asked if he should fly home from Asia. I was blessed by so many.

I'm also thankful for the wonderful weather we had this fall, allowing me to lie on the deck and rest. Maples turning the most beautiful shades of red or orange and yellow, catching my gaze and causing me to look once more. My courage, which rarely fails. A church family who prays for me and visualizes healing and wholeness. Friends, patients, and blog readers who are cheering me on. My painting and writing, which give me purpose and keep me focused.

I'm glad to be one of the luckiest people on earth. Glad for a great life, too.

While celebrating the first Sunday in Advent, and anticipating the birth of the Christ child, I remember that God does his best work in the dark. He's working that best in me now.

Peering into the shadows, I seek light. And when I find it lying in a lowly manger, I am reborn. I've heard this story before, and it does not end in death or blackness. I'd be a liar if I said it did. I just had to be reminded.

Message: Sometimes hospitals give inadequate, or even dangerous, care. I'm sure most of you know of a poor outcome in the inpatient setting. In this case, my nurse was arguing with my oncologist and refusing to take care of me in the simplest ways. It was torture. Her poor nursing support led to a two-week infection that was so painful

I couldn't speak or walk. Fortunately, my husband reminded me of all I had to be grateful for, and I turned my song of lament into gratitude. Gratitude in the midst of severe suffering is powerful. Sing a song when you are in your gravest situation, and God's blessings will compound.

The Twenty-One Club

A SIX-BY-NINE-CENTIMETER LESION. Twenty-one lymph nodes removed, twelve positive. Stage IIIb. I am just now admitting the size and number of these lesions, the diagnosis.

At the time, not believing it was happening, I hid the seriousness of my cancer and the prognosis from everyone, including my husband. I believed that if I spoke the awful facts out loud, they would become true. So I stayed silent. I couldn't stand when people looked at me as if I were already dead. Even now, when I return for my yearly checkup, the looks of incredulity at my vitality remind me how fortunate I am, how miraculous each day is.

When the research coordinator came to enroll me in the clinical trial, she had a multitude of questions. Most of them were simple. But I'll never forget how my oncologist scrolled down the computer screen until she found the pathology report, and pointed when the research coordinator asked my diagnosis. They gave me a copy in a brown envelope, and asked me to call with questions.

"Julia, read this, and we can discuss it at your next visit."

We never had a meeting to discuss the report.

In two years of treatment, no one on my team ever spoke the results out loud. I read that report silently, in the sacredness of my bedroom.

Prior to my surgery, I commissioned a portrait. It hangs in my bedroom, and in it I am holding a prayer shawl while a hummingbird extracts cancerous growths from under my arm. The ninety-first Psalm graces the background. My head is bald, but my breasts are intact.

"If you'll hold on to me for dear life," says God,

> *"I'll get you out of any trouble.*
> *I'll give you the best of care*
> *if you'll only get to know and trust me.*
> *Call me, and I'll answer,*
> *be at your side in bad times.*
> *I'll rescue you, then throw you a party.*
> *I'll give you a long life,*
> *give you a long drink of salvation!"*
> —Psalm 91:15-16

And instead of weeping, I had a party and shredded that report. It had nothing to do with God's expectations for my life. Certainly, it had nothing to do with my plans.

While I sat and prayed, I heard a confident voice assuring me, "I'll show up and take care of you as I promised, and bring you back home. I know what I am doing. I have it all planned out. Plans to take care of you, not abandon you. Plans to give you the future you hoped for." (Jeremiah 29:11)

Message: When you are trying to visualize yourself healed and complete, it may help to minimize the facts, depending on your personality. When I was in medical school, a study revealed that being told the mortality, morbidity, and other statistics about a procedure decreased some patients' anxiety and increased it significantly for others. I am in the group that wants to know less. Consider how much knowledge will benefit you and tell your doctors.

Twelver

ON MY FOURTH FOLLOW-UP after the surgery, the extractions were over, the drains out, and the infection cleared.

My surgeon looked at me. "I want to see you in a year. How about October, breast cancer month?"

I looked at him. "Will I be here that long? Long enough for a one-year follow up?"

Replying with bravado, my surgeon referred to me as a *Twelver*, and said to his nurse, "We've had Twelvers who make it over a year, haven't we, Patty?"

He was referring to the number of positive nodes out of the twenty-one he'd removed.

This diagnosis? I saw her holding back words of death. Wanting to speak, but not able to agree with him, she said nothing.

I left the clinic without making an appointment, not because I thought I wouldn't make it one year, but because I never wanted to see either one of them again. I am a human being, not a *Twelver*.

Message: You can choose when to dismiss a doctor. While I was grateful for the surgery, the lack of professionalism created a chasm between me and my surgical team.

Radiation

EAGER TO BEGIN RADIATION SO I COULD FINISH by Christmas, December 25th was my goal. For eight months, I'd been hearing what a "piece of cake" radiation would be after all I'd gone through.

In retrospect, this may have been misplaced enthusiasm, because I was sick and weak. My expectations were skewed because I had done so well with the chemotherapy.

I started the radiation before the raging infection cleared, and I was optimistic I would finish by Christmas.

"Thank God the infection is on my left so we can proceed on my right, cancerous side," I told my husband, the night before my first visit to the radiation clinic.

On the initial consult, they tattoo you—make two permanent green dots on your chest and under your arm so they can line up the radiation beam precisely. I have heard survivors compare these tattoos to the ones given in concentration camps, but I never saw them that way. Instead, they were beacons of light reflecting the transformation of my body. Now, when I catch a glimpse of them in the mirror, I remember God's promise to prosper me with long life. I'll take that promise and live.

There were thirty treatments total. A mat was applied to my chest, intensifying the radiation to the skin since the cancer had already spread. After twenty rounds, my skin had melted. What was left was an erythematous (red), layer of ooze that burned. I begged them not to finish the last week.

A lovely invention by a burn unit doctor saved me—a thin white gauze material that could be cut to fit, and adhered to my wounds. Breathing like skin, it felt like a hand of mercy, and enabled me to work and function. I protected that side of my body, making sure no one touched or bumped into me. By the third week, I was fatigued and ready for bed by midday.

While praying and listening to a meditation tape during the lasering, I directed the beam burning my skin to destroy only cancer cells. I thought of the bright light and loud buzzing noise accompanying those treatments as the light and thunder of Christ, soothing my body and diminishing primitive cells. Despite that meditation, I ran out of steam, patience, and hope, and I limped through the last days.

Enduring two treatments a day the final week allowed me to finish on Christmas Eve. I celebrated with twelve women who had supported me since March 21st. We ate and drank champagne after toasting the year past and raising a glass to the next.

Message: Milestones are important and should be marked. My support group joined me Christmas Eve to celebrate the end of traditional treatment. They encouraged me regarding the next phase. It was fun and exciting to be with the women who had facilitated my journey. I was surrounded by love.

The meditation tape I played during radiation relaxed me and gave me hope. It also drowned out the buzzing noises. Jesus' beams lit up my body and the room.

Statistically Speaking

"Who Care What the Numbers Say?-"Statistically speaking, my mom didn't have the luckiest year. But who cares about the numbers. I would be hard-pressed to find a smarter, cuter, more perfect mom."

Wilton, my daughter, wrote this birthday message, her love and confidence echoing.

Nutrition

And then came another avenue of healing—a plant-based diet and a change in lifestyle.

While I was riding a stationary bike at the health studio, Stuart, the owner, said, "Julia, I've got a person you should meet."

"Who?"

I was bald and flat, so everyone knew.

"A friend who practices Ayurveda medicine—a nutritional and hygiene regimen."

"I'll give her a call. Where does she live?"

Turns out, she's a neighbor. And three months later, after changing my diet to organic plants, freshwater fish, and lean white chicken, I've embarked on a journey that defines my daily routine. It transformed me, and I can't imagine my life without these rituals.

Months later, I'm doing a two-week cleanse with a mono-diet of rice and mung daal beans. Ayurveda delineates three energy types: *pitta*, or fire; *kapha*, or water/earth; and *vata*, or wind.

"All disease is caused by a separation of mind, body, or spirit from nature. Life must be lived in concert with circadian rhythms and the seasons."

Thus, I purify and cleanse my body during seasonal transitions. Awakening early to sit with the rising sun, eating my biggest meal during the middle of the day, and being asleep by 10:00 p.m. are daily habits.

I don't remember when I started the journey toward imbalance. Was it shortly after birth, while wasting away, allergic to all the formulas Momma tried? Or was it in college, while practicing the piano hours each day? Or maybe in medical school, when I had anatomy lab six days a week?

I admit to imbalances. Disavowing both spirit and intuition in favor of science and logic, I suppressed my creativity while training to be a doctor, and later while practicing as a psychiatrist. I couldn't play piano for years during and after medical school. There were so many imbalances I've stopped counting. It doesn't lead to equanimity.

But Ayurveda does. I've surrounded myself with healing

creams, and drops made from flowers and herbs, which I put in and on my body. I believe in my ability to right this ship if I honor my body with organic food and holy routines. I believe in this three-thousand-year-old practice intuited by sages.

Message: After treatment, so many people will have advice for you:
"You need to relax."
"You better not eat meat."
"Julia, you have to eat some red meat, or you will get anemic."
"Don't drink."
"A few drinks here and there will help you feel better."
On and on the litany goes, until you absolutely have to pick something— paleo, vegan, vegetarian—and stick to it. I chose Ayurveda because it made me feel better so quickly. In about seventy-two hours, many of the side effects from my treatment went away. You have to find your own way without being too influenced by others.

Tree Healing

ONE DAY, I WAS READING a book on alternative healing, and I decided to tell my stories to a tall birch tree. I hoped to lift these imbalances and my illness to the sky, through the tree's branches, and bury them in the ground through its roots.

That birch listened to all the stories I cared to tell that day—some remembered, others forgotten, all truths spoken out loud.

After the birch tree promised not to break our holy confidence, I thanked it for the long session.

Talking to a tree lightens you and clarifies your thinking. As a daddy long-leg climbed across my arm, I gave thanks to God for blessing the stories and the cleansing.

Message: There are many modalities for healing. Chose the ones that make you feel better, and commit to them daily. Reading the Bible was one for me. Reciting the ninety-first psalm with my daughter right before bed was important as well. If she was away, I played an audiotape of her recitation. Find rituals and healing Bible verses that support you. It is also fun to experiment with alternative exercises, like talking to trees.

Depends on What You're Offering

LAST WEEK, A MAN AT THE THEATRE GAVE ME A GIFT. It was my first night out on the town since the diagnosis, and my daughter and I were going to the symphony. Walking down the aisle, with a fuzzy head, I was trying to find my seat. I found it, five rows in front of my daughter's.

As she peeled off, I yelled, "Hey, Wilton! Meet in the lobby at intermission."

With a hand cupped around my mouth, I spoke much louder than a whisper, right into a man's ear.

He turned and looked. "Wilton?"

"Yes. Is that your name, too?" I replied.

"No, but it could be. Depends on what you're offering."

In that brief, rude interlude, we laughed deep in our souls, and I was recreated feminine—not a cancer patient, or a woman without hair or breasts. Not a number in a clinical study, or 12857, whose blood counts were measured weekly. Certainly not a woman who is afraid to live and be appreciated.

His laugh, his light, the obvious pleasure he took in that joke, created a living testimony that despite all the treatment and dehumanizing experiences of the year, I was worthy of flirtation, still desirable and sparkling. As his words wrapped around me in splendor, we held still for a single second. He will never know the moment that passed between us. I will never forget.

Message: Even though it was sexist, this man made me laugh and feel good about myself. I liked that. Be with the people that appreciate you. The ones who tell you that you are still beautiful. The ones that love you, and you love back. Have fun.

Anniversary

HARD TO BELIEVE IT'S ALMOST THE FIRST ANNIVERSARY of finding the infection that turned out to be cancer. One year since that long day which turned me upside down. Ten hours of testing, after weeks of antibiotics, became a year-long sentence of treatment, even as the *I can't have cancer. I'm going to Hong Kong to see my son*, litany trailed. The trip that never materialized was replaced by chemotherapy, radiation, surgery, and lots of pain.

From: Jennie, NP
Subject: Affirmation
Date: March 21, 2015
To: Julia Burns

My one year affirmation for you is the butterfly. Symbol of joy, grace, lightness, change and powerful transformation.

I hope this is a positive image for you. Also - I love the hibiscus flower. Attached are a few photos of the hibiscus in my yard this week - amazing! I hope you have a relaxing weekend,

Jennie

Message: The one-year anniversary of my treatment was another milestone. We celebrated and reveled because we were still together. My daughter's love shone through the day. Celebrate your victories with those you love. Although your year may have been filled with pain, and your body ravaged by the treatments you received, you still have much to be grateful for. You are alive.

It's Up to You

AND AT THE END OF THAT LONG YEAR: "You've managed the physical, Julia. Now it's up to you to manage the mental," said my sainted husband, the one who'd nursed me all year long.

He had no desire to live with an invalid.

My body was ravaged. I could barely lift my arms over my head. My fingers and feet were numb. My arm swelled and ached and my scars screamed. I was a tangled mess.

Despite being good at managing others, I knew I had to keep working on myself. Pilates, yoga, tennis, walking, lifting weights, acupuncture, massage, lymphedema massage, therapy, Rolfing, physical therapy, and stretching. And now, a clinical trial. After that long year of traditional treatment, chemotherapy, surgery, and radiation, I was ready to enroll in the clinical trial. A drug, Everlimus, had shown promise in reducing metastasis in renal cancer. The hypothesis under investigation was whether this effect could generalize. This trial would shed light on that.

The head of oncology—the one who'd answered the

email, and later the telephone, when I was bleeding in ambulatory care—suggested I enroll in a double-blind study.

"I think you should do it, Julia. There's a chance, if you get the active drug, that it could make a difference. We have to throw everything we can at this."

And what could I say but, "Yes, I think so, too."

So after hours of instruction, measurements, and orientation, I was enrolled. There was a dietary restriction on grapefruit juice and grapefruit. Apparently, it deactivated the drug's effect.

"Thank you for the new drug. And I'll be sure to eat grapefruit for breakfast every morning," I sang, as I tripped out of the drug study office.

She came running after me, explaining for the tenth time that grapefruit was not allowed.

"No worries. It was a joke," I said, but she wasn't laughing.

After a few days on the Everlimus drug study, I knew I had received the active drug and not the placebo, because of the side effects—blisters in my mouth, an itchy rash covering my body. The blisters were supposed to go all the way down my GI tract, but they didn't.

Grateful to be alive on this one-year anniversary, I sing thanks again for my family, friends, church, doctors, the drug trial, and especially for Jesus' pure white healing light. All difficulties lend themselves to love.

"Doesn't this feel fantastic," and "Hey, I'm still alive for this moment," I say to whomever will listen.

Happy anniversary, inflammatory breast cancer. You have changed my life for the better, and I thank you. We are in this together.

Message: Although it was disappointing to be dealing with difficult side effects, I was grateful for the opportunity to participate in the drug trial. I still haven't heard any results, and the itchy rash and sensitive skin were extremely unpleasant. When faced with difficult decisions, like whether or not to participate in experimental drug trials, consult your doctor and listen to your God.

Another's Death

"Faith is the assurance of things hoped for, the conviction of things not seen."

—Hebrews 11:11

LENT STARTS NEXT WEEK, and I am ripe for ashes on my forehead as I think about death—mine, others' and Jesus'.

Last night, Maggie, a friend of my daughter's, came to the house in tears. Her neighbors had been killed—a man, his wife, and his sister. They were engaged in a fight with another neighbor about a parking space. All were pronounced dead at the scene. Don't bother to call the ambulance or do CPR. Don't panic that you're losing pressure on that chest wound— their deaths were immediate.

Before I got the news of this shooting, I was writing about my death—my own and Jesus'. However, in the face of this vengeful hate, my writing turned. How could it be that these two women will never have a baby and breastfeed, or perhaps get cancer at fifty-seven?

A tremendous hollow swelled in our chests as they released photos. Nineteen, twenty-one, and twenty-three—a dentist, a dental student, and an undergraduate. The killer is in custody, proud of his accomplishment, of ridding the world of them.

What mental health treatment could have prevented these deaths that was not available or was too expensive? Who knows what maltreatment he suffered as a child that created such fear? And the realization came that in the scheme of things, my death is insignificant.

The media focused on the murdered man's Twitter feed. He and his wife were Muslim, and he had just written, "killoing Jews or killing Muslims is futile. It won't help." And yet his own death came as the very sacrifice he spoke against, creating more insanity and grief.

Hoping the deaths of these three young adults would count for something better than the chaos created by that gun or the disputed parking space, I prayed to God to make it so.

Message: In the face of your health crisis, you will become aware of life events that tragically surpass your own trials. It will take you away from yourself and into the world. Praying for your town and the troubles found there is good because it reminds you that you are needed. You are still an instrument of God's peace.

Betrayal

WHILE WATCHING HOME MOVIES of our young family playing games, shooting bows and arrows, laughing and reading together, I was struck by how I was always nursing.

After watching my daughter latch onto my right breast, I turned to my husband.

"That is the breast that betrayed me."

"Ah, but hasn't it done so many wonderful things as well?" he replied.

And I had to admit that it has. It doesn't seem fair though that a middle-aged woman should endure a year of treatment for a cancer that had spread through her body like a detonated bomb, so destructive that intense treatment, followed by a clinical trial, may not be enough to save her. It's not fair that her internist treated her cancer as an infection for weeks, instead of referring her to oncology, who didn't call for another week, when that lost time could mean the difference between life and death.

Faith that goes forward triumphs, and no matter how dearly I wish time could go backward, it never will. So I choose to walk in this moment, forward with my God, hand in hand, without fear.

Message: Often, we have doubts, and second-guess our course of treatment. This is a good time to refer back to Psalm 91, and remember, "He shall give his angels charge over you to keep you in all your ways." God is always watching out for you and trying to assist you. Believe in your present, and don't dwell on the past. Walk hand-in-hand with God. He has something special planned for you.

Up from the Grave She Arose

IT'S NOT THAT I DON'T BELIEVE. I do. It's just that I doubt, too. As a scientist and doctor, I have to doubt.

Holy week highlights the relevance of life after death, a crucifixion ending in resurrection. As a flash of light energy runs through my body when the congregation rises and sings, I'm looking for renewal and rebirth. As a Christian, I declare my faith in a living Lord. Thus, how can I fear death? Where does my belief in miracles begin, and where does it grind to a screeching halt?

How is it easier to believe that Jesus was nailed to a cross, stabbed with a sword, forced to swallow vinegar, taken down and buried, before rising on the third day, than to believe that my cancer will be eradicated? That in combination with medical treatments, there will be miraculous healing by the Holy Ghost?

If Jesus healed the woman who bled for twelve years (she had only to touch his robe for it to happen), then can I touch Jesus' robe and be healed, too? Why did Mary doubt, days later at the garden tomb, when she found the stone rolled away, the body gone? She wept while Jesus watched her, and she said, "Where have they taken him?"

And where are they taking me?

Some days, I don't want to go there. Death is the ultimate trip, only you don't need a passport. The destination is well-known, and getting there inexpensive.

How can I believe Christ's story, and not my own? I don't want to live as renegade cells take over my body, establishing dominance, weakening me and destroying my organs. I don't want that for my family, either. Going out in a flame suits me better.

"What springs from earth dissolves to earth again, and heaven-born things fly to their native seat," said Marcus Aerolius.

If I am dissolving and flying to my *native seat*, I want it to be swift and clear, not messy.

Stories about cancer deaths invade my thinking, and I push them away hard. Whether or not God heals me physically, He loves me every day. Healing is based on the laws of the universe and God, not my beliefs.

Because I can better comprehend the exquisite beauty of life, spring assails my senses in a unique way. Green leaves unravel more slowly, birds sing loudly and urgently—listen here, listen now. A sparrow resting on three eggs in a planter just outside the front door waits by the Japanese maple's red curl, squeezing my heart gently in a place I didn't know existed. And I am in awe, not that I might be dying, but that I was ever privileged with living.

Message: You will have days where you dwell negatively, and days when you rejoice. Accept this, because the dark days will meld into sacred days of gratitude. Sometimes it may feel like a roller coaster. Hang on and try to sing the praises of the One who put you on this ride.

Innocence

"IT'S A WILD ANIMAL SAFARI OUTSIDE, Mom," Wilton said, as I walked in the door.

I gazed out the sliding doors and saw a red fox chasing a mother deer and her baby into the creek. Back and forth they went, until the mother escaped. But the baby was stuck in the water. The fox leapt over rocks to cut off her path. Afraid of water, he waited on the bank, stalking, content for the deer to die of fatigue or hypothermia.

Their dance reminded me of my struggle—one minute, you're grazing in the grass. Then a predator finds you, and you're running and squealing, struggling to breathe. Jumping into what you think is a safer place—chemo, surgery, and radiation—you pray that the disease chasing you cannot swim and will walk away soon.

"My God sent his angel, and he shut the mouths of the lions. They have not hurt me, because I was found innocent in his sight." (Daniel 6:22)

Daniel walked out of the lion's den, unharmed. I am walking out unharmed, too.

Message: "I was found innocent in his sight." (Daniel 6:22) There is nothing you can do that God will not forgive. God loves you, and when you ask for forgiveness it is already there, waiting. He loves you beyond your humanness. If God had wanted perfection for company, he would not have created flawed humans.

Another Biopsy

"Though he fall,
he shall not be utterly cast down,
for the Lord upholdeth him with his hand."
—Psalm 37:24

THREE WEEKS AGO, as I awakened, my fingers grazed a hot, tender, raised node. And then I found another, and another. Three of them were there, where yesterday there was nothing. And the positive thinking, the sure way toward healing, slid away, choking off possibilities of mother of the bride, and babysitting for grandchildren.

"How fast will this go? How much longer? You mean, I only got four months out of all that?"

After easing out of bed, I sat on the deck and sipped tea, watching the sprinkler circle the garden and create a rainbow. The garden was planted last spring, the spring of the diagnosis, the season of treatment. Each planting is in memory of Momma, and in honor of two college graduates— Owen and Wilton. It was slow going. Two minutes of digging, one for seeking plants. Then resting. Finding ferns, hostas, hellebores, peonies, Solomon seal—the yard so full of treasures eager to settle into a new creation.

And now, sitting by this garden, watching as a magic rainbow ascends and descends in the sprinkler's mist, I wondered, *What God? What message is in these colors? That you will not destroy your children? That you are not destroying me?*

I planned to go to the hospital alone. My husband was

flying with the boys to San Francisco, for a Grateful Dead concert—a present for nursing me all year. This news would spoil the surprise. But I was scared, and hesitated. I ultimately asked my cousin Rick to drive me.

Punch biopsies hurt, and I wanted to take a pain pill. Plus, I needed the company—someone to keep time in the waiting area when they sent me away after checking my blood pressure because they didn't have an empty patient room. Someone to feel the injustice as I waited for hours while they located a setup tray.

I guess they forgot you were coming, Rick texted.

Finally, the setup tray was located, and the nurse practitioner finished her work. While tying my stitches, she asked me to schedule a follow-up.

"Are they doing immunotherapy for IBC?" I said. "My friends aren't ready for me to die."

Tears slid down our cheeks as she told me that immunotherapy was not working against breast cancer.

I tried to think of anything but the biopsy report—gratitude for each day, each minute, each second abounded. While I waited at the beach for the results, my daughter visited, bringing fellow oceanography students. They were scientists who mostly didn't believe in God, and definitely didn't believe in religion. Their doubts echoed ones that I no longer entertained, since I had struggled for years with God about sexual abuse. It was a fight I didn't win. And even in the face of death, I was sure that God was good.

Their youth, their lackadaisical manner and incessant grumbling over their jobs derailed me. Gazing into their vibrant faces as they leaned into each other with joyful laughter scared me. It hurt to feel their intense energy.

"Hey, you better pay attention, because you never know— look at me. I may be dying," I wanted to say. But of course, I

didn't.

Those burning, swollen nodes haunted me, shadowed my days, making me remember what I was trying to forget.

"They said you talked about God too much, Mom. Really! They all knew you were religious, but that was different."

Then I told her about the nodules. "The biopsy report came in negative—fibrous tendrils."

Wilton asked the same thing I had asked the nurse: "What is that, fibrous tendrils?"

"Scar tissue," the nurse had replied. "I thought someone let you know yesterday."

I had been waiting all week to hear. How do they lose a pathology report? Especially when someone is waiting, sitting by her phone for a call that will release her so she can skip to the beach, whole again?

While listening to the nurse's voice on the phone, I felt strange, submerged, numb, and disbelieving. But *scar* it is, and scar I'll take, and live.

"I thought I was dying," I said. "I had been waiting six days for a pathology report when your friends arrived. If I seemed different, off-balance, it's because I was. I'm sorry if I talked too much about God."

She nodded, tears sliding down her cheeks, because technically she already knew. Our thoughts wandered back to the second I found the nodes, and my phone lit up with her texts.

How are you, Mom? How are you feeling? What's happening? she texted, as my fingers strayed, exploring those swellings.

Even though I tried not to tell, she knew. The secret never really was. That's the way it is between us, always.

"It makes me feel like what Dad and I did all year doesn't count when you talk about God healing you. I just want things to be the way they were before."

"Oh, honey, you have no idea how much I want that, too."

I tried to explain that if I'm preparing for heaven, a place I have to go without her, then that changes everything. It makes me less of this world.

"Jesus is the rock on which I lean, but that doesn't mean that you and your Dad aren't important. Everything you did for me counts. You are the hands and face of Jesus, but nothing in this family will ever be the same."

Truly, she's more scared than angry. But hurt and anger are easier than anxiety. And as we muddle through, and I silently place Christ between us, I ask for a blessing on our love, even when it comes in fear.

Message: Fear. Of course, fear sets in when there is danger. Certain that those hot nodules meant metastasis, I panicked. That the oncologist had the pathology report for a day and didn't call made it much worse, as if I didn't count. My daughter's anger at my growing attachment to God is understandable in light of feeling like God was taking me from her. There was much to process, and no good way to do it. Prayer was a first step.

Sharing the Good News

From: Julia Burns
Subject: Biopsy
Date: June 30, 2015
To: KP, HS, JW, SG PH

It was two fibroids showing no sign of carcinoma. God has rescued me once again.

Julia

From: Kathy
Subject: Re: Biopsy
Date: June 30, 2015
To: Julia Burns

Praise God from whom all blessings flow! Thank you for sharing this wonderful news.

KP

From: Jo Anne
Subject: Re: Biopsy
Date: June 30, 2015
To: Julia Burns

God is so good. Praise him for this tremendous news. Thank you for sending this to us.

JAW

From: Pat
Subject: Re: Biopsy
Date: July 1, 2015
To: Julia Burns

Yes! Yes! God is our faithful Father! Here is the scripture I had for you today before receiving this email: "Do not fear; those who are with you (us), are more than those who are with them." 2 Kings 6:16

PAXPLH

Bless Me First

"I will not let you go unless you bless me....
Then he blessed him there."

—Genesis 32:26,29

WHILE STUDYING THESE WORDS, it dawned on me that Jacob ended his fight with the angel not by wrestling, but by clinging. Magnificent faith was required to give up the struggle, to trust and cling. Weary from the fight, he relinquished to the victor, not by letting go or giving in, but by persistent clinging—clinging until he was blessed.

While working as medical director at a child welfare agency, I was shocked by the stories of abuse, and got angry. Angry at the perpetrators; at the State who started treatment too late; at the treatment center who punished negative behaviors, but didn't honor trauma stories; at God; and at myself because I had to listen day after day, but couldn't change anything.

"I could have done better, Lord. Anyone could have."

Eventually, after much debate and wrestling, a more mature understanding of the insidious, pervasive presence of evil led me to stop wrestling with God. But I do still cling.

Clinging, praying for mercy, I wait until I receive my blessing, and even then I am reluctant to let go. There will be a time for release, but it will come later.

Message: While singing in the praise band, I realized God was clinging to me, and that I could let go. *When the night is holding on to me, God is holding on.* He placed me with traumatized children so I could listen. He put me exactly where he wanted me— where I could do the most good. He even graced me with a blessing and forgave my anger. And then he healed me.

Prosthesis

AND SO IT HAS COME TO PASS that this brazen, confident, honest-to-a-fault woman has come to a precarious place. A place of truth or fake. A point of real and less than real.

If I want to have breasts, I have to wear a prosthesis. My bilateral mastectomy left me bound by scars and flat, almost concave.

Research during the initial days of my diagnosis warned that reconstructive surgery for IBC was ill advised: "Too aggressive. Close monitoring is imperative. No reconstructive surgery until later."

So even as the earnest, young residents broached the subject, I ended it with, "I'm not eligible. My cancer is too aggressive."

That silenced them. Doctors rarely talk about aggressive or death.

I glance in the mirror and see my lower ribs protruding past my chest, and I am painfully aware that my symmetry is off—way off. On some days, I go flat. And on others, I wear an obscenely expensive prosthesis. Insurance reimbursed the vendor $10,000 for two bras with pads. Ten thousand. Yet they denied the eighty-five-dollar claim for a compression sleeve, reminding me of the days when Medicaid reimbursed for Viagra, but not birth control pills, and changed their policy only after women revolted. I feel like revolting, too.

With my fake breasts, I appear much like I did pre-mastectomy: curvaceous and *normal*. Fake breasts look better because even at sixty, they don't sag. My friends are envious. Male eyes brush my cleavage with surreptitious glances, until I want to say, *"Stop. They're foam rubber."*

We all have choices. We can be fake or real, and I'm not talking just about bosoms.

Message: Something about living with cancer and its harsh treatments for two years made me feisty, and edgy. I laugh at the men who steal glances at my prostheses. They seem influenced by an age-old instinct.

You may find yourself getting quieter and more agreeable, or perhaps more spirited. Celebrate the new you and try not to judge. Go with yourself and discover new ways of being.

Love your Cancer

KELLY TURNER, IN HER BOOK *RADICAL REMISSION,* advocates nine key factors for cancer survivors: radically changing your diet, taking control of your health, following your intuition, using herbs and supplements, releasing suppressed emotions, increasing positive emotions, embracing social support, deepening your spiritual connection, and having strong reasons for living. She challenged me to ask my cancer what it wants, what lesson it is trying to teach.

"Love your cancer because it is lonely and requires loving attention."

Western medicine teaches us to fear cancer, to eradicate, eliminate, poison, radiate, and surgicate.

"Listen to your cancer. Ultimately, it is trying to heal you, to teach a noble truth."

Ummm, I guess so. I ponder these words as my scars constrict in black pain, and I sit inside on beautiful sunny days because this experimental drug makes me allergic to the sun.

Early in my illness, my sister casually said, "We can't hate it, Julia. It's part of you."

I remember being shocked. Not hate my cancer? I tucked the thought far away, but it came back as I read about a survivor's hypothesis that love for his cancer was the key element in his return to health. Deciding to listen to my cancer, I asked what lessons it had for me.

Many healers believe that emotional roots are connected to diseases. Victimization, resentment, and anger are often associated with cancer.

I was sitting with two friends at a local barbeque grill and jazz bar, eating kale, when they said, "We've heard that cancer is related to marital strife."

I laughed. "I'd be the last to deny that my husband and I don't have strife. Of course we do; we're married. But look at you two. You are both divorced, and you didn't get cancer. Surely there was resentment and victimization in your marriages. All people in relationships have conflict. It's how we negotiate conflict that creates love. Your discord resulted in physical and mental health issues, too, so I don't think it's helpful for cancer patients to be called repressed and angry. It seems simplistic to blame cancer survivors for being resentful caretakers."

The precise message I received in prayer about this was: *We should not work at forgiving, because it is already forgiven. You cannot be betrayed, because I have taken that betrayal from you before it happened. This includes forgiving ourselves.*

This knowledge pierced me deeply. Could it possibly be that easy—quit trying so hard and lay down resentments because they are forgiven before they occur?

And just in case I didn't receive the message fully, the sermon that Sunday was on forgiveness: "You don't have to forgive, because it is already forgiven. God loves you."

On the way home, the Baptist marquee read, "Love makes enemies disappear."

If I listened correctly, I am charged with increasing joy in my life and bringing it into the lives of others. Who knew it could be so easy? And why do we make it so hard?

Don't let your friends confuse you with accusations of what you did or did not do to get cancer. Look ahead at the mercy and love of God. Of course you have resentment and hard feelings. You are human. Friends that point fingers are afraid. They erroneously believe that if you harbor ill feelings and they don't, that somehow they will be healthy.

Message: Kelly Turner has made a career out of documenting survivors and their methods. Be curious, try loving your cancer as she suggests, and see what happens.

Another's Death

DURING OUR HEALING SERVICE, we prayed for a young man, Michael, who had lost his parents in a car accident. I struggled with this news mightily, determined to find meaning in this tragedy. It was a while before I realized that I was over-identifying with Michael because my daughter and I were caught in the same struggle.

My email to my prayer partner read:

> From: Julia Burns
> Subject: Ah ha
> Date: Sep 28, 2015
> To: Pat
>
> Good morning. It took me until 9 p.m.
> prayers to realize that the reason I was
> so moved by Michael's parents' deaths
> is that my daughter and I have been
> wrestling with the same thing. Duh!
> Thanks for letting me say it out loud.
>
> Julia

From: Kathy
Subject: Re: Ah ha
Date: September 28, 2015
To: Julia Burns

I love how God continues to work out in us his truth and wisdom as we meditate on the words and thoughts he brings to us when in community. He is so dependable to fulfill his purposes for us. He delights to share his wisdom! Beautiful! So glad your schedule allows you to be at our healing service on Sunday afternoons!
KP

What's Left?

"WHO IS THIS IMPOSTER HIDING IN MY SKIN?"

I want, and I don't want. I'm so relaxed that I volunteer to sing praise songs, and could care less when I miss a note.

"I was singing for my Lord. That's all that matters," I tell myself.

My estrogen blocker is blocking my emotions, too. I hate it. I don't mind the joint aches and pains, but I miss the emotions. I can't feel joy when the wind rustles leaves and they drift into the creek. My daughter's phone calls don't bring happiness. I can't laugh at my husband's silly jokes. I recognize that I should be feeling something, but I don't. I'm a shadow of my old self, and I miss what used to be me.

Now that the traditional treatment is further behind me, and this treatment progresses, I wonder, *What's left? And what got left behind, forever?*

> **Message:** It is normal to feel left out and to feel lost. My anti-estrogen left me feeling empty and achy. I didn't recognize myself, and I missed the vitality I had cherished. I kept trying new medications, but nothing worked. The bone pain was intolerable, and I couldn't move well. My oncologist promised a 50 percent reduction in relapse, but I found I couldn't live with the side effects.

Say Yes

SUNDAY NIGHT, WHILE PERFORMING with the praise band, I desperately sang, *"In the middle of the storm, I am holding on to you."* As I lifted my arms in thanksgiving, I remembered that God is the one that clings, not the other way around.

The whole week, as I floundered in fear and dread, He was hanging on tight.

I wrote this prayer in response to that epiphany:

> Dear God, make me a grateful and obedient servant to do the work that you have chosen for me. If I am to be sick, make me patient, loving, and kind to those who care for me.

Give me gratitude for those who work to heal me, and mindfulness to remember that I will not be sick forever. Encourage me to seek all modalities of healing, including intercessory prayer, healing prayer, and meditation. I grant you sovereignty in the creation of my life, accepting my pain and suffering with humility, knowing you are watching over, holding me close as I experience this deep adversity. In the name of Jesus, the great healer, I pray. Amen."

Message: God will always say yes to what He has promised.

Burn that Bush Again

I'M AT THE BEACH AGAIN, reading the litany of healing from the prayer book, remembering fondly my days at the Episcopal convent. Each Friday, after packing the children off to school, I departed for silence and prayer.

"Remember when you used to go to that monastery, Mom?" my daughter said.

"Yes, I do. And when you have three little children, you'll be running to silence also."

It was at the convent that I saw the burning bush outside my window early one morning in late fall. I peered out, looking for my future, and beheld a blazing small bush. Most people in my life did not believe in my burning bush. That did not deter my hope.

Did that miracle exist, or was it the slant of light from the sun blowing red, reflecting the leaded window from which

I gazed? Now I'm looking everywhere for miracles, and God grants them in the rotation of the earth around the sun, falling stars, hearts beating, the implantation of a fertilized egg that becomes a baby.

Memorizing the healing litany for a sick friend, I intoned:

> God make our bodies a temple of your presence. Grant your healing grace to the sick, lonely, anxious, or despondent. Give us knowledge of your will, and awareness of your presence. Mend broken relationships, bless healthcare providers. To the dying, grant peace and a holy death. And by the grace of consolation of your Holy Spirit, uphold those who are bereaved. You are the Lord who does wonders. Amen.
>
> "A Litany of Healing"
> from *The Book of Common Prayer*

Make my body your temple, Lord. Lift me up and burn that bush one more time. Please, God, I'm scared. I'm not scared. I need to know your plan.

Message: Often it is the uncertainty of the outcome that drives your fear. And your fear drives your ruminations on death and goodbyes. I believed in the miracle of the burning bush, and I believed God set it on fire to get my attention. *You will live, Julia, and do something amazing.* I wondered what it was.

Peru

SITTING UNDER A SKYLIGHT, writing for the first time in weeks, I'm struck by the spinning whir of the washing machine. I am bathed in joy and happiness to be exactly where I am—home.

Having returned from a trip to Peru, which was transformational, I sit in gratitude for both the time away and the place to which I have returned. *Hold that conversion,* scatters across my consciousness as I remember the challenge: The only moment that exists is the one I am in.

Listening to the machine's whine lessen and stop, I am grateful for dirty clothes and the ability to wash them while I write.

While in Peru, I walked through the symmetrical plumb walls of Manchu Picchu. I bent over and placed my hands in two bowls—concave rocks hollowed by the Incas for watching the moon and sun. Winded, my breath came easier as I felt the water lapping around my fingers. Other tourists mimicked my gesture, and I laughed, knowing they had no idea why they followed, even as I had no idea why I'd bent over in the first place.

Riding a horse along a flowing Urubamba River, I felt the power and compassion of that animal as we galloped through the countryside. Days later, running across the heights of a valley filled with salt pools, I soared.

Once we returned to our accommodations, I lay in the grass and saw a cloud engulfing me as a flock of black birds flew over. Later, during yoga, a vision consumed me as a lion strolled up beside and roared in greeting. We gazed into each other's eyes in curiosity, rejoicing in his message *I've got life.*

"So have I," I replied.

The following day, I drifted through a floral labyrinth, contemplating an eight-hundred-year-old lucuma tree. So much fecundity in a myriad of colors surrounded me as I walked that maze, it seemed that secrets and entreaties encircled my every prayer for health and a full life.

Blowing in the wind, a purple petal brushed my arm as I continued in holy circles. I believed the flowers were awestruck by my presence, too.

On the day I traveled to Peru, a terrorist attack killed one hundred thirty people in Paris, and wounded 494. The attackers, armed with assault rifles and explosives, targeted six locations across the city. It was the only news reported in the airports from home to the sacred valley. The horror and finality of their deaths inspired a sense of oneness between the victims and our group; the atrocity represented a societal cancer.

November 16, 2015, 11:29 p.m.

I Love. I Am. You Are.

On the first day, she said, "All that I am, you are, and all that you are, I am."
We breath in and we breathe out as the tragedy of hundreds of French music lovers unfolds in a concert hall. They are groaning goodbye to their loved ones. All they wanted in that moment was to hear the cello wail, but it was silenced, too.
On the second day, she said again, "All that I am, you are, and all that you are, I am.

But I still didn't want to believe.
We breathe again, in and out, honoring the
killers with the black suicide vests,
the dark powdering of bullets striking lives
and scattering hopes.
On the third day, she said, once more, "All that
I am, you are, and all that you are, I am."
Breathe in, breathe out as the hummingbird
flies into this blossoming,
healing ourselves as we heal the world,
becoming all of you and all of I.
There is no escaping this.
As we meld into a space of wonder, the in
breath sighs, and the out breathe follows.
I mark it, making an even bigger opening in
my chest where I know my heart weeps
but also sings with joy as the hummingbird
dances above me every morning.
Remember, all that I am, you are,
and all that you are, I am.
Bowing to my own seeds of aggression, hatred,
and bigotry, I take a breath, breathing in light,
love, beauty, wisdom,
and the knowledge that
you and I are one in Christ.

"I may never go back. I don't want to be anywhere but here," I said to the emerald green hummingbird that hovered over every morning.

Yet I knew, when the time came, I would be ready, able to take this love and healing back into my everyday life. The life I would never leave. The one I love more than any other.

Message: When you are sick, you worry that life will never return to normal. You wonder if you will be able to do simple household chores, travel, or enjoy dining out. Life stops, and so do you. This trip was a godsend from a friend. She made sure I paced myself and had fun. Believe your health will be restored, and you will enjoy a full life again, including travel.

Stairway to Heaven

PADDLING ON MY BOARD FOR THE FIRST TIME since the diagnosis, balancing is difficult, and that's why I'm doing it. Hovering above the space and place I love most—the Bogue Sound—I spy dolphins breaking the plane of the water, and try to emulate their grace. It eludes me.

A former patient of mine died this week from cancer. A few months ago, he was in Thailand organizing technology, writing software programs. When he returned, a headache came and never left. Soon, an MRI came back positive. So strange, isn't it, that bad news in the medical field is a *positive* result? A positive brain scan in this case meant four tumors.

He and his wife were having trouble keeping up with their schedule—transitional problems from fulltime work to being home. They were having difficulty loving each other while juggling endless trips to the doctor for surgery, radiation, and chemotherapy. His wife came in like an organized CEO of a Fortune 500 company, managing more appointments in a month than most folks have in a lifetime. She did it with grace and accuracy as he suffered through countless intrusive treatments, even though he'd been told, "Go home, meet with your attorney and financial manager. The location, size, and extensiveness of the metastasis deem a poor prognosis."

We sat together, and I said, "Why do you get so upset when folks leave the house and it's not on the schedule?"

"I don't know," he replied.

So, I tried again. "How long are they gone?"

"Not long. Not long at all, really. I don't know why I care so much if we follow the schedule."

"If they aren't gone long, and you don't really care, why the upset feelings, the angry outbursts?"

"I don't know."

"How long is not long for you?"

"Not long. Not long at all."

"Do you think you get angry because you are afraid that you will die before they return?"

"Yes. I do think that."

I turned to his wife. "See, he's not angry because you can't keep the schedule. He is angry because he is afraid he will die before you return, and he will not have time to say goodbye."

That put the situation in a different light.

After he spoke the truth, it seemed natural to ask him what he will miss, what frightens him.

He sat there and looked me straight in the eye. "Their birthdays. Missing my children's birthdays."

His honesty took my breath. I'd expected him to say, *"I want to see them graduate from college and get married,* or, *"I'd like to hold my grandchildren."* But instead, he said, "I'd like to celebrate the twins' birthdays with my wife." And I knew he knew, because those birthdays were less than a month away. He understood what no one else in the family could. No wonder he was trying to control the schedule.

"How is your faith life?" I said.

As he struggled to answer, I said, "Rapidly advancing?"

We laughed together at the joke because we could; we were alive and it was funny.

Later that month, he had a seizure and the doctors had trouble stabilizing him. When I visited him in the ICU, he woke up just as I entered his room. He was squeezing the nurse's hand on command, and moving his foot. And then he squeezed mine. Looking miserable, he gazed up at me, pushing down with his right hand in an urgent, emphatic way. In answer, I recited several Psalms—23rd, 91st, and 121st. Then I sang the song of Mary and "I'll Fly Away."

"I promise to help your family in every way possible," I whispered.

Visualizing a stairway moving from his bed, upward, I watched angels guide his family and him toward heaven. I placed my hand on his forehead, blessed him, and then left.

As I waited for the elevator, I was hyperaware, all five senses buzzing. Even now, I vividly remember each person standing nearby with overnight bags and flowers. I wondered, *Are they being discharged to recuperate? Or are they holding the belongings of a deceased loved one?*

Walking to the parking garage, I absorbed every color, sound, and emotion as people walked by, towards, and away from the hospital. Climbing into my car, I turned on the radio, and *"Stairway to Heaven"* was playing. Rolling around the ramp of the parking garage, I sang loudly as together we built his stairway to heaven.

Message: Lying there with tubes and monitors and no chance of getting better, he waited, and so did we. Make sure your living will is in order. I wanted a strict Do Not Resuscitate. I don't mind dying, but I do mind endless, futile suffering. Sitting with patients who were dying of cancer when you are sick might appear difficult, but it wasn't.

Praise Band

FOR YEARS I'VE DREAMED THAT I AM IN A ROCK BAND, belting it out on stage, applause deafening, only to wake up to my normal life as a psychiatrist. Some part of me must have clung to the dream, because when our praise leader asked for volunteers, I waited until no one stepped up, and then approached.

"I know lots of hymns, and I sing in a gospel choir," I said.

Years later, I am still singing with the praise band on Sunday nights, so I must have passed the audition.

"*Breath on me, breath of God. Breathe on me. God resurrect these bones. I come alive, I'm alive when you breathe on me.*" I waltzed around the house, singing, until my husband knew every song too.

But before rehearsal, I was in great pain, and I bowed in prayer to ask for healing. Rashes covered my body. I was itchy, hot, stiff, achy, and mentally dull. It seemed to me that I had suffered enough, and that the time for complete healing was now.

Complaining to God, I said, "My timeline, Lord, not yours."

After asking my prayer partners to join me, we prayed for peace and calm in the storm of these reactions to the study drug. Kathy, one of my prayer partners, saw me lying at the bottom of a deep, dark hole, dressed in a white robe, while Jesus performed CPR. She saw me receiving the breath of the Holy Spirit.

"Breath on me, breath of God. Breathe on me. God, resurrect these bones. I come alive, I'm alive when you breathe on me."

After the service, we laughed together at the synchronicities between the words of the song and her vision. Singing those lyrics on stage, asking God to breathe on me, it felt like Jesus *was* doing CPR. She didn't know the words to that song, or the ones we planned to sing, but she did know God's heart.

> **Message:** Thanks be to God for breath that sustains, and for friends with prophetic and healing powers. I come alive when he breathes on me. Find prayer partners that pray over you and increase your faith and hope as you come alive.

Eternal Love

BROKEN, YET BEAUTIFUL, the shell I've picked to commemorate Valentine's Day is cracked and fragile, imperfect, yet eternally durable. I transported it to the house and placed it on a glass shelf. It sits there still, reminding me of my brokenness and my durability.

Two years ago, my husband and I were celebrating St. Valentine's Day at the beach when he noticed my red, hot breast.

"You better have that checked out, Julia."

But I thought it was an infection, and so did both doctors I saw, giving me one round of antibiotics after another that helped but didn't cure. Finally, I stumbled into the oncology clinic after reading about inflammatory breast cancer (IBC).

"Pretty sure this is not me," I said, "but I think someone should take a look."

Cancer has robbed me of so many things. I did not want it to rob this year's Valentine's celebration, too. But I felt edgier and grumpier with every mile as I drove towards the beach. Angst filled the car, until dread for this day of love was all I felt.

I called several friends in the prayer group. "Please pray for me. Bless me and this holy day of love. I'm sinking."

"I pray that God heals your memories around this most lovely, romantic weekend. May God use this Valentine's weekend to remind you how He always brings forth life, light, and love, making beauty from ashes, and rebuking evil and darkness, especially darkness that wants to kill, steal, and destroy your happiness. Praise God, who redeems everything. And Julia, I mean everything."

And just like that, it was gone.

"This is Valentine's Day, 2016, not 2014. There is no such thing as cancer or darkness."

It turned out to be a spectacular day of love, with candy, roses, candles, and a card. A day of love, not death and curses. A day of healed memories, not sadness and loss.

Message: Thanks be to God for his infinite love and wisdom, and for prayer partners that pick up their phones when you call. Find yours so that when your courage and hope fail you, they can remind you of God's redemption for all circumstances. "So now faith, hope, and love abide, these three; but the greatest of these is love." (1 Corinthians: 13:13)

The Truth about Cancer

WHILE WATCHING A MINI-SERIES on the cure for cancer, I am struck by how little I know about alternative treatments. For years I have said that the cornerstone of a cancer cure was going to be prevention through nutrition, lifestyle, and exercise—all aimed at decreasing chronic inflammation. Simple techniques which alkalinize pH balance and boost immunity will prevail. Still, traditional medicine refuses to consider "alternative" techniques as the rate of cancer in America increases and is higher than in most developed countries. Research funded by drug companies supports chemotherapy, surgery, and radiation, so they remain mainstays of treatment.

"These treatments release stress hormones which can exacerbate or spread cancer cells. They also deny the reality that stem cells are present in the blood stream no matter how small the tumor. Therefore, the myth of 'we got it all' is deadly," say experts on Ty Bollinger's *The Truth About Cancer*.

Ty's experts discuss alternative therapies, including organic whole-food diets, electrical pulsing, essential oils, and supplements such as iodine, curcumin, ashwaganda, and amla. Therapists demonstrate emotional release therapy. The toxicity of ungrounded electrical fields is emphasized: "Ground your digital electronic devices. Don't put your cell phone near or on your body. Turn your Internet off at night. Put it on a timer," says Chris Wark of *Square One*.

Chris, a Christian and long-term survivor of Stage III colon cancer, has established a program about cancer prevention and treatment. Ty Bollinger also researches and explores alternative treatments in *The Truth About Cancer*: "Resist the urgency for surgery that your doctors mandate. The cancer has been in your body for seven to eight years by the time it forms a localized tumor. A few weeks to research your options will not increase metastasis."

The use of cannabinoids (CBDs), the non-psychoactive component of the marijuana plant, is recommended. Also, the psychoactive component of the marijuana plant, THC, has demonstrated effectiveness in ameliorating effects of chemotherapy. THC for untreatable brain cancers has been reviewed and found to be effective in shrinking tumor growth in some cases.

CBDs increase bone density, treat insomnia, depression, and anxiety, and have fewer side effects than many toxic prescription drugs. Studies done by the National Institute of Health, conducted in Israel, show that CBDs stabilize dementia and can *reverse* it. They decrease the symptoms of multiple sclerosis, fibromyalgia, and intractable pediatric seizures. The use of CBD oils and salves are a regular staple in the management of my pain, burns, and adhesions.

"Why did you prescribe oxycodone, steroids, and NSAIDs for me when CBDs were available?" I said to my nurse practitioner. "NSAIDs create leaky gut and malabsorption, steroids depress the immune system, and oxycodone is addicting. How can you prescribe toxic drugs when CBDs are legal, available, more effective, and create less side effects?"

She listened carefully, but could say nothing, as THC was illegal, and CBDs were taboo.

On another visit, I questioned her about nutrition: "How is nutrition considered alternative?" I mourned the lack of information over the two years of treatment.

Fresh organic plants and lean white meats, lightly sautéed, steamed, or roasted, without salt, sugar, or butter: these things comprise my diet now, but I gleaned this information on my own by perusing the Internet. I never received any nutritional information from the hospital and staff.

I am grateful to my traditional oncology team for the work they did to stabilize my health, but I wish they were curious about non-traditional treatments. Thanks to Ty Bollinger and Chris Wark for the illuminating insights that aid me daily.

> **Message:** Be bold in your search for alternative treatments. Discover your path and pursue the treatments that make you feel whole. Don't wait for your doctors to enlighten you. It probably will never happen.

The Sacred Plant

From: Kathy
Subject: Hi, Julia
Date: March 21, 2018
To: Julia Burns

Have you ever seen this series before, *The Sacred Plant: Healing Secrets Exposed?*

My sister says she has, and I am just catching up to the background on CBD.

It feels a bit propaganda-ish, but I decided to step through it because I know nothing other than a general sense that CBD oil is helpful for a variety of conditions.

KP

From: Julia W. Burns, MD
Subject: Hi, Julia,
Date: March 22, 2018
To: Kathy

Yes, I have a hilarious story about
this. I tuned into Ty Bollinger and
The Truth About Cancer when my radical
traditional treatment was finished. I
knew I needed to maximize my chances,
and felt it was time to turn to
alternative treatments. Last spring, Ty
started promoting *The Sacred Plant* series
and since I had followed his advice
on many subjects—essential oils,
supplements, water, and nutrition—I
decided to watch.

I posted his Sacred Plant link on my
website and Facebook.

I had NO idea it was marijuana. Ha-ha.
So a few nights later, I'm sitting on
the sofa, watching The Sacred Plant,
and realized that the sacred plant was
marijuana. I jumped up and took down my
advertisements lickety split.

However, I did continue to watch all
seven episodes, and I've done lots of
research.

. . .

...

I use CBDs daily now. When I run out, my pain is so awful. I don't know how I survived without them. Big believer. I keep this story quiet. Only word of mouth with trusted friends because my main story is God, healing, and child sexual abuse. I don't want confusion. CBDs are legal in all fifty states, and medicinal THC is legal in twenty-eight states. They work so well for many things; it's only a matter of time before medical marijuana is legal in America.

It's often the only thing that works with intractable pediatric seizures and inoperable brain tumors.

Also, the NIMH has been conducting research in Israel with CBDs and THC on dementia, and it's showing stabilization and reversal.

I find it fascinating that we live in a society that continues to produce, sell, distribute, and market oxycodone, which kills sixty to seventy thousand people every year, and yet passes laws to incarcerate people for growing and selling marijuana, which has so many medicinal properties and couldn't kill you if you took a truck load. ...

...

I am praying into this and happy to
speak with you. Definitely watch the
series. Yes, their propaganda is over-
the-top and off-putting, but science
backs them up.

Julia W. Burns, MD
JuliaBurns.org

God Gets Credit

*And when he called unto him his twelve
disciples, he gave them power against unclean
spirits, to cast them out and to heal all
manner of sickness and all manner of diseases.*

—Luke 9:1

I GIVE GOD ALL THE CREDIT for healing me, but none of the
blame for making me sick.

"How can that be? Isn't it both or none?" folks ask.

Wondering at a heart and mind that conceptualizes God's
grace for healing, but not the responsibility for sickness, I
affirm that God did not create sickness or evil. Creation of
free will led to disorder and chaos, and it has been man's
decision to nurture and increase chaos, disease, and natural
disasters.

Cancer is the ultimate expression of disorder and entropy—undifferentiated cells refusing to mature, so in their primitive state they replicate unchecked. This devious ploy can end in death, and is a parallel process of how evil governs: Act natural, act normal, deceive, and dominate. Then once you are in control, destroy.

God gets no blame for evil or disease because it does not belong to him. We hold that blame ourselves when we pollute our water and earth, destroy the ozone, and poison our food with pesticides, preservatives, and genetic alterations. God gave us the garden of Eden; we gave him destruction. And then we blame God when illness strikes. All these problems exist, but I do not dwell on them, because miracles and healing happen every day.

"They did not receive the things promised. They only saw them and welcomed them from a distance, admitting that they were foreigners and strangers on earth. People who say such things show that they are looking." (Hebrews 11:13-14)

After Jesus and the disciples healed the masses, some of those healed ran in fear. Others gathered in astonishment, hoping for a cure, too.

I crawl to the Master like the hemorrhaging woman, and stretch out my hand to touch his robe as he walks through the crowd. I desire to transfer just enough healing power, and no more—not running in fear, but standing strong.

Prayers of gratitude flow continually from my heart as he tells me to be patient, to allow more time for the scars and adhesions to soften, for burns and restrictions that bind my chest to heal. Paintings fill my studio as I sing, *"Praise God from whom all blessings flow."* Outside, the garden blossoms anew. Shoots thrusting from the ground trust the sun for adequate nourishment, and although millions of miles away, the sun warms the earth with the light needed for rebirth this spring.

Message: Be astonished. Ask for healing and expect a miracle. We must trust God's love as it creates wonders every day. Open your arms to receive all his blessings.

Looking Forward

RECENTLY, I WAS PRAYING WITH A CANCER PATIENT, hovering my hands above her bald head as I repented of any hardness of heart I harbored about my own illness. Blessing her, her courage and stamina, her strength and desire to live, I called her cells into order. I asked Jesus to hold dominion over every cellular function, muscle, tendon, and electrical impulse in her body.

"Give her courage to enter the chemotherapy suite and pray over the life-giving toxins that will be infused. Let them target cancer cells, and leave healthy tissue alone. Bless her family during this trial, especially her children. Please God, cover her children. And thank you for answering this prayer, even as it leaves my lips."

"I used to want to scream at folks when they told me that one day I would find this time to be a blessing," I said. "But it happens. This disease converts into something you appreciate, something transformative. Eventually."

I was confident in my healing by the Holy Spirit, and I was confident in hers, too.

"I'm looking forward to that," she said.

"So am I."

Our God is looking forward, too.

Message: I grew confident in my ability to pray over people with diseases. You may decide to engage in healing prayer, either as a receiver or giver. God appreciates it when we pray for others, transforming the circle of life.

The Lesson

MOST PEOPLE DID NOT KNOW the seriousness of inflammatory breast cancer, but they were still curious as I started growing hair and glowed with good health.

"How are you, Julia? You look amazing," they would say.

"I decided to listen to my God and not my doctors," I replied.

Their questions sparked my interest in speaking about healing miracles.

I taught an adult education class: "How comfortable are you when you hear, I was healed by the Holy Spirit? How many individual healings did Jesus perform? Do you believe demonic forces were present in Jesus' day? How about now? Does evil have power over individuals or groups? Is the Bible the word of God? Did these miracle and healing stories really happen, and could they happen today? Is healing alive and relevant today?"

We pondered these difficult questions together.

One of the ways I made healing real during my year of treatment was to pick a story from the New Testament and engage directly with the character, making her story my story. The one that spoke to me was the woman who hemorrhaged for twelve years and crept toward Jesus, seeking to touch his robe. Having sought the advice of many doctors, she spent much money trying to find wholeness, without success. But as soon as she touched his robe, she felt the bleeding stop, and she knew she was healed. Jesus turned and said to his disciples, "Who touched me? I felt the power leave."

Both Jesus and the woman knew instantly that something amazing and wonderful had happened. I felt it, too, as I knelt and prayed for God to save my life.

> **Message:** Healing is immensely personal and real. Each one of us is a gifted, creative artist, made by God, in his image, and we can activate healing in ourselves and others. Healing is the ultimate gift of God's creativity. How do we encourage this gift? How do we thank him for it?

Fear

Though he slay me, yet will I hope in him.
—Job 13:15a

ONE DAY, AFTER TEACHING A CLASS ON HEALING, I got sick. My arm swelled and felt numb. The pain was deep and unrelenting. It occurred to me that saying my diagnosis and discussing the treatment out loud with others caused fear, which in turn caused pain. Panic set in as I answered questions about dying—who does, and who doesn't.

"How do you know you are really well?"

Even as they asked, the computer screen showing the statistics for two-year survival rates flashed into my head.

"None of us knows if we are well," I replied. "But words from the Bible remind us that it is by peace and calm that we will know him."

Yet when I finished the lecture, the pain was so intense that I grabbed two prayer friends and asked them to speak words of healing.

"Dear Lord, we speak life and vitality over Julia, not death and fear, pain and tightness. Ease her swelling, Lord, and reduce all inflammation in her body. Help her remember that you give relief as you release her now from this darkness that came over while she was speaking about miracles and healing. Lord, we praise you for this resurrection. Amen."

Message: Wanting to share my growing belief that prayer was an effective modality for healing, I began speaking to others about my experience. Having kept the pathology report and severity of my illness quiet for years made this more difficult. It felt like I was breaking a code of silence that had kept me safe. Since so many people survive breast cancer now, I felt the need to explain the extent of my disease and the dismal survival statistics. But I got caught up in others' doubts, and it made me sick. Prayer and turning to God for relief changed my attitude and physical response. Make sure you have prayer coverage when you speak with others about your illness.

Truth and Lies

DEAR BRENT,

I just finished reading *Everything Happens for a Reason: And Other Lies I've Loved* by Kate Bowler. Thank you for suggesting it—just so well-done. I truly loved it, and the writing was terrific. I could, of course, relate to most of her stories. I was greatly heartened by her disdain for our current medical system. I've also had medical crises in my life when I was seeking diagnoses and treatment, only to be turned away by "experts." I really admired the way she took the gloves off and pelted them. I was struck with how she said, "I'm not leaving this office until you order another test. I'm sick."

The part that made me cry most was the end—things not to do, and things to do. "How are you, really?" is my least favorite question, especially as it usually comes in a public forum, where there is no possibility of an honest response. *"Who knows?"* I always want to say. But in my heart, I know the answer is, *I am well. How are you?* The Creator who made us and every living thing, holds me in his hands—before cancer, now, and after death. I put all my faith in that.

The part that made me the saddest was her lack of faith that God does cure—inexplicably, and perhaps from our view, capriciously. But he does, even when we don't expect it, or have any hope that it's possible. She does not embrace this, despite so much evidence to the contrary in the New Testament and the present. Thus, she is missing a great opportunity to represent miracles to a world deeply in need of healing.

I sent her a copy of *Radical Remission* by Kelly Turner, when she was diagnosed. It's a spiritual, but not religious, book about thousands of cancer survivors from all over the world—Stage 3-4, with and without traditional treatment. It delineates the nine things these folks have in common—fascinating and hopeful. I keep copies of it and pass it out when a friend or family member asks for help with a newly diagnosed loved one. You can never pass out too much hope.

While I'm on this topic, I would say the thing that exhausts me the most about being a cancer survivor is the constant pain and infirmities I suffer as a result of my treatments, past and present. I can't feel my fingers or feet, so I drop things and I'm clumsy. I'm in constant pain from my incisions and lymphedema. My joints ache, and I can hardly walk sometimes because of a pill I'm afraid not to take because they assure me of improved survival.

And who, as Kate so beautifully says, doesn't want to stay in the Now? It's exhausting, and friends, and even family, can't imagine me in this deep pain, so they refuse to do so. Leaving us somewhere in between a place of life and death and disconnection. Some days, I relate to her desire for a definitive end.

Not many days am I so dark, but the residual, the life they've left you, is so different from the person you imagine or remember—as if you're living in a stranger's broken body. You're grateful, but you miss yours. You miss normal. You even miss all traces of normal memories.

While I want folks that love and live with me in this life I've brokered and bargained and pleaded for, to remember this, I don't want pity or quick asides such as, "That's too bad," or "Julia, how is your health?" But I do want them to remember how much I hurt and how not a single day goes by that I don't wonder if I'm dying, and *Who will help my daughter put on her wedding dress if not I?*

Four years ago, I sat in a room with my husband while six providers looked down at their feet, one of them mumbling something about *keeping me comfortable*, and I screamed "No!" The odds of me being here, writing this email, were slim. I had less than a 25 percent chance of living two years with Stage IIIb Inflammatory Breast Cancer, a rare and aggressive breast cancer—it's a miraculous healing.

I live today through and by God's grace, mercy, and the healing power of Jesus Christ, with a little help from traditional medicine.

Following a plant-based diet keeps me that way. And of course, I continue to beg and pray, rarely lifting, "Thy will be done," in reference to the saving of my life, but rather, "Save me today, God. Take this swelling, this pain, this numbness today."

I won't be joining your book club, for obvious reasons—too close. But I do appreciate you, this book, and this chance to celebrate healing miracles, including Kate's and mine.

Love,

Julia

The Beginning and the End

THE LIFE OF A PSYCHIATRIST CAN BE ODD. Today, seven patients were scheduled. Two late-canceled, two no-showed. That left one who got sick, and two who came.

No-shows were rare during the first decade I practiced medicine—probably no more than three or four. But the chaos of summer, and the mores of 2018 combined to create long moments of sitting in the sun and listening to the creek's meandering, bird songs tumbling from tree tops, and bees zumming, hard at work as I sat quietly. Contemplation came also—more than is typical for a meditating healer.

A lovely woman who sought healing prayer revolved through my mind. She came for prayer, and pray we did, earnestly, fervently, and with deep conviction that God's will would prevail and healing would happen. I had seen so much spiritual, physical, and emotional healing, including my own, that I forgot to ask God his intentions. I wanted what I wanted, and failed to remember that I was merely a channel of His light.

On the day of a follow-up MRI, she came asking for prayer. This MRI would determine her response to chemotherapy and if she were eligible for further treatment. She was so scared she could hardly sit as we lay hands on her and beseeched God to cast out cancer and fear. We prayed for peace for His will, and for the terror to subside so she could enter that loud cantankerous machine that was to determine her future.

Although I prayed for His will, I didn't mean it. I thought I did, until she died. And then I questioned. Didn't her children need her? We pondered the truth of her diagnosis and prognosis as we interceded.

"Don't listen to your doctors. Listen to your God," I told her, confident that she could outlive their damning prognostic predictions, as I had.

We met for coffee and talked about wigs, cannabinoids, our children, and death. She knew from the beginning that she was dying, after two months of bleeding, while the doctors told her nothing was wrong. And she knew, as her daughter scolded her when she violated her vegan diet that was supposed to cure her. She knew, even as we prayed over her. But I denied.

So when the text came that she had died, I struggled. No matter how many times I extolled the mysteries of healing, and how God always works miracles—sometimes physically, often spiritually, but He always heals—I was stuck. Refusing her death, I questioned the God I loved and worshipped so freely.

My simplistic theory, which I didn't even know I held until the message came, was that if it worked for me, it would work for her. Wasn't she brilliant and capable? Didn't she have myriads of friends pleading, and hundreds praying? How could doctors at two leading cancer hospitals work on her case and come up with nothing? Couldn't God just grant one reprieve in a universe so filled with mourning and lamentation?

But no, He didn't save her physical life. And then after I questioned God, I blamed myself. Why hadn't I gone to the hospital to pray? Why hadn't she asked for me to come? God hadn't done enough. I hadn't done enough. And if we had pulled together, we could have lifted this mighty weight and created life.

When death came, I discovered that the answers that seemed so evident in theory lacked everything in practice. And so quietly, while on my knees beseeching him, God reminded me that His way was good enough, big enough, sufficient enough, and that questioning only deepened confusion and pain.

"Be still and know that I am your God, even if it doesn't always make sense," He whispered in my ear, as I hung above the creek, rocking in the hammock.

This I took as truth, both His and mine.

Message: I took what was God's job and tried to make it mine. When I heard about her death, I doubted myself, healing prayer, God, and her doctors. It was a terrible time of struggle and denial. A time of beseeching God for understanding, while on my knees in regret, suffering, and confusion. God greeted me with a different message: *Be* still and know that I am God. Be still and know that I am. Be still and know that I. Be still and know that. Be still and know. Be still. Be. (Psalm 46:10)

Goodbye Song for a Friend

The sea is pounding.
Silent doves are mourning.
Yellow daffodils sent by an angel messenger
greet me on my morning walk,
as even the evergreens bow
in wonder at her beauty.
The time is long.
And yet the sun at day's end sinks
silently past a horizon which welcomes her
with arms wide open,
as the moon rises full,
shining light on us and her life.
Joined in this moment,
where the rising and setting collide,
we weep at this leave-taking.
Wanting her with us forever,
we thought it should be,
and now that she lives in a place in-between
that seems so far away, we long.
Receiving a transformation
that even nature rages against,
my dear friend sighs at last, in resignation,

as moonbeams illumine a path that lies
uneasily by the edge of the ocean,
and we stand by her side, protesting in fury,
singing, holy, holy, holy.

—Julia W. Burns, MD

About the Author

JULIA W. BURNS, MD HAS
WORKED as an adult, child
and adolescent psychiatrist
healing trauma for over
thirty years. She studied
music and psychology at
the University of North
Carolina-Chapel Hill and
medicine at Wake Forest
University Medical School.

Julia's first book, *Momma,
Who's Babygod?* shows how
prayer and the Holy Spirit can influence parent-child
dynamics. Julia's experiences with childhood trauma in her
role as Medical Director of a three hundred child welfare
agency led to her highly aclaimed book *Songs for the Forgotten*.
She has published articles in Buddhist and trauma survivor
magazines.

Julia deeply believes that all wounds no matter how
severe can be healed and demonstrates this in her books and
healing practices.

Connect with Dr. Burns at: www.juliaburns.org
Facebook: drjuliaburns
Instagram: @doctorjuliawb
LinkedIn: julia-w-burns-md-478b9071

Endnotes

1   Greg Guthrie, ASCO staff. "2019 National Cancer Opinion
    Survey: Americans Need More and Better Education about
    Cancer Prevention, End-of-Life Care, and E-Cigarettes,"
    October 30, 2019.

2   Burstein, Brett, MDCM, PhD MPH1, Agostino, Holly,
    MDCM2, Greenfield, Brian, MD3, "Suicidal Attempts
    and Ideation Among Children and Adolescents in US
    Emergency Departments," 2007–2015.

3   JAMA Pediatrics, 2019;173(6):598-600. doi:10.1001/jamape-
    diatrics.2019.0464

CPSIA information can be obtained
at www.ICGtesting.com
Printed in the USA
JSHW041321290421
14090JS00003B/114

9 781611 534016